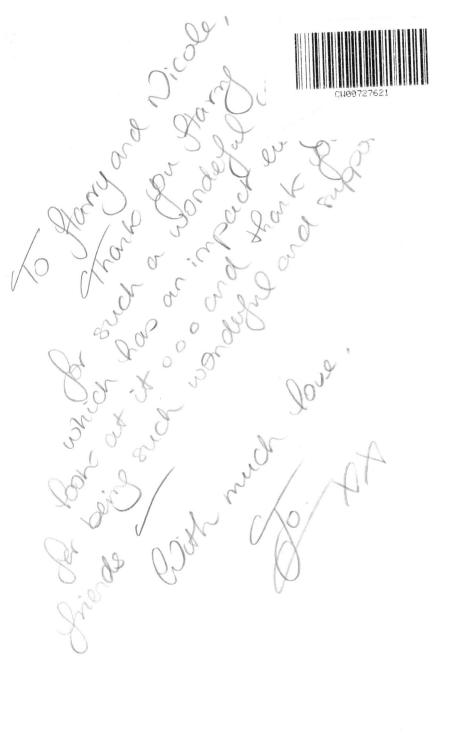

To Harry and Nicole,

Thank you for being such a wonderful c...

which has an impact ev...

been at it ∘∘∘ and thank ...

being such wonderful and sup...

friends ✓

With much love ,

Jo xx

CN00727621

# Our Dark Twin

The Paradoxical
Saviour Within Us

By Joanna Lehmann

Tagman

www.tagman-press.com

# Our Dark Twin

First published in hardback in 2005 by The Tagman Press, an imprint of Tagman Worldwide (Ltd), Lovemore House, 5 Caley Close, Sweet Briar Estate, Norwich NR3 2BU, England UK

Internet: www.tagman-press.com
E-mail: editorial@tagman-press.com
Telephone: 0845 644 4186

ISBN: 1-903571-56-1

Cover design by Lippa Pearce Ltd
Illustrations by Joanna Lehmann
Design by Amanda Lehmann and Lippa Pearce Ltd

Printed by Lightning Source, UK Ltd, 6 Precedent Drive, Rooksley, Milton Keynes, MK13 8PR, Bucks

Tagman

Tagman Worldwide

# Dedication

*To my parents Ann and Vic, my sister Amanda, Steve and all the friends and spirits who have given their support and inspiration.*

# Contents

## Part One: The Essential Nature of the Dark Twin

## Part Two: Venturing into the Dark Twin's Realm

# Introduction

## The Inspiration for *Our Dark Twin*

Ever since my late teens I have been on a quest for truths that exist beneath the surface of our lives, and which illuminate the paths we choose to take on the journey of life. Increasingly, I noticed how the interaction of opposite forces drives the positive changes and revelations we experience.

During a traumatic period, I had dreams about the way in which the paradox of life at its deepest level is linked to encountering and facing the darkness. For instance, I would seek the source of spiritual music in the top of a cathedral spire, but would not find it until I had descended into the crypt. The answers and revelations were never found through attempts to either rise to the heights of a spiritual place or to escape from a terrifying situation; they were always found beneath in the depths, or at the hub of the blackness. I discovered that others had received similar dreams at times of emotional turmoil, and that if they heeded them, then positive change took place. I realised that these revelations linked with the most powerful myths, such as those of Inanna, Persephone and Dionysos, where in each case growth and transformation occur in the deepest part of the Underworld. This was strongly reflected in books I read by people like Brian Keenan and Helen Keller, who had received deep insights, enlightenment and hope in the grip of the darkest of circumstances, and who were subsequently able to impart their inspiration to others. I noticed how friends could become so much stronger and more able to release their personal power when they had dealt with hardship and the source of their pain through facing its challenge. A pattern had emerged.

As I began *Our Dark Twin* I set out to present the force that enables us to break through the walls of conscious repression as a multi-faceted personality and the Spirit of a universe that runs parallel to our worldly existence and provides the deeper resolutions to its problems. This spirit of pain, grief, the unconventional personality, the "shadow", is also our potential and our link to universal knowledge and inspiration. It encompasses all the fear-inducing, dangerous, but powerful dynamics that paradoxically can also save us, leading to new levels of strength, creativity, illumination, and the realisation of the authentic self.

Through focusing and linking the various aspects of the underside of our personal lives, *Our Dark Twin* aims to be of value to those seeking meaning and a sense of deeper purpose in life, those who have encountered darkness, or those who are suffering and looking for solutions.

# PART ONE

## THE ESSENTIAL NATURE OF THE DARK TWIN

The Dark Twin's Power

# THE DARK TWIN'S POWER

*The demon that you can swallow gives you its power...*
Joseph Campbell, *The Power of Myth*

There is a point where one archetypal Dark Twin exists, in the centre of all things.

His breath is the air we breathe from the moment we leave the light of consciousness and enter the subterranean realm. His bones are the walls of winding passages and yawning caverns. His voice is the rumbling of the earth as it shakes the very roots of the Underworld itself. His heart and soul exist in the form of a fierce beast we meet in the central core of the Darkness. This monster challenges us to overcome him and to conquer him, to both revere and embrace him. We tame him to harness his energy. We finally absorb the essence of his power, and we then go through a metamorphosis. It is through solving the riddle at the heart of this contradiction that we are liberated and empowered with new life.

The Dark Twin resides in the subterranean realm of our unconscious. He has many sides. He is androgynous, for he can be either male or female. He is the negative force of greed, ignorance, selfishness, hatred, jealousy, cowardice and entropy. He is the Shadow lurking in the inner recesses of our psyche. He is explosive chaos and wild ecstacy, animal instinct and aggression, the Trickster, the Outcast, Death and Transition. He also unlocks the door to new experiences and adventures, thereby expanding awareness and growth, and he opens the way for the expression of our desires, our inspiration, our creativity, our personal development, and our deepest feelings of love, compassion and spiritual insight. The Dark Twin is a paradox we ignore at our peril, and he exists within each and every one of us.

It is not easy to be prepared for an encounter with this inner spirit. It takes courage, faith, awareness and balance. In *Seventy-Eight Degrees of Wisdom*, Rachel Pollack states, "Those who allow the unconscious energy within themselves to emerge, guiding it with love and a faith in life, will discover that the energy is not a destructive beast but the same spirit force drawn down through the lightning rod of the Magician." The Huichol Mexican tribal people go yearly on a pilgrimage to meet their Great Spirit, but they say that if they are not strong enough, the spirit kills them. On the other hand, they believe that if they are prepared, they then enter a state of ecstatic fusion with life and return home having discovered their lives.

The Dark Twin is the shadow aspect of the Great Spirit of which we are all a part. It is his darkness that gives birth to the Light of our spiritual victories. We may perceive him as a negative force we wish to avoid, and he is potentially dangerous and destructive, but it is he who opens the way for our development and liberation as human beings. He gives us the power of transformation.

*Twins of Darkness and Light*

# TWINS OF DARKNESS AND LIGHT

… in silent darkness born.
Samuel Daniel

Day gives way to night, and night to day, summer falls as winter takes over, and winter makes way for summer. The force of Darkness initially appears to be in direct opposition to the force of Light. However, as we look deeper we see the layers of truth unfold to show an intriguing twilight area that reveals the magical tapestry of Life, where the two forces are woven together. It is a truth that has been understood and expressed through mythology and the ancient mysteries for many thousands of years. Ancient deities display both the different manifestations of the Dark Twin's character, and the way in which this power not only contrasts, but also connects with the force of Light in a deep paradoxical mystery.

Essentially the Dark Twin is the character of the Underworld of our lives and experiences, and therefore each aspect of his character has a counterpart who represents elements of the Upper-world.

For the Ancient Greeks, Dionysos, the wild god of wine, excess and the irrational was the dark brother of Apollo, golden god of the sun, culture and reason. It was understood that they were opposites, but that one could not exist without the other.

For reason, ruling alone, is a force confining; and passion, unattended, is a flame that burns to its own destruction. Therefore let your soul exalt your reason to the height of passion, that it may sing; and let it direct your passion with reason, that your passion may live

12

through its own daily resurrection, and like the phoenix rise above its own ashes.

Kahlil Gibran, *The Prophet*

The connection between Dionysos and Apollo is also reflected in the eastern concept of Yin and Yang. Here, balance only occurs when these two forces of opposing factors co-exist in equal measure. This truth was expressed most strongly through an understanding of the nature of Dionysos and Apollo at Delphi. For the ancient Greeks this was a holy site of prime importance, situated at what they believed to be the centre or "navel" of the Earth. Apollo was the god of the great temple here, but the worship of Dionysos took over for the winter months. The Pythia, the famous Delphic oracle, gained her inspiration from fumes of a vapour rising from the ground. So, Apollo's oracle depended on a gift from the depths over which his dark brother presided. It is here that the mystery deepens to reveal an additional connection.

The name "Pythia" came from "Python", a snake that in mythology Apollo slew when he took over Delphi from the ancient Mother Goddess. He was only able to take control if he incorporated the spirit of the old earth mysteries and religion, of which the snake, the oracle and Dionysos as the twice born fertility god, were a part. With his personal experience of death and rebirth, Dionysos had the snake with its regular shedding of skin and its semi-underground existence as one of his symbols. As the snake had rejuvenating and medicinal powers, it was also the symbol of Aesclepius, the god of Healing, who was closely associated with Apollo, his father and mentor. The similarities between the two supposedly opposite deities went further than that. For instance, both were connected to the arts, for Apollo was god of culture and music, whereas Dionysos was god of the theatre. Both were musical; Apollo was associated with the lyre with its spirit energy, while Dionysos with his nature energy was often depicted with the panpipes.

Dionysos and Apollo both contained feminine qualities. Dionysos was sometimes depicted as androgynous, as for instance in Euripides' play *The Bacchae*, in which in a wrathful mood he sends his female followers into frenzy! Apollo was one of the few Greek gods to express sexual interest in someone of the same sex. Between sexes the distinction is never completely black and white. Men and women contain elements of each other's gender within themselves, for each needs an aspect of the other to be a fully developed human being, and to form successful relationships based on empathy and mutual understanding.

This deeper layer in the mystery of the nature of opposites is also depicted by the Yin and Yang symbol, for on the dark Yin side there is a light spot, and in the light Yang side there is a dark spot. As A. Baring and J. Cashford write, "Each contains the other in embryo". Each contains the seed of the other and each gives birth to the other. Night and Day is an example of this process. We sleep during the night so that we have energy for the day, and the day gives us the experiences that feed our soul and our dreams at night, which in their turn prepare us to deal with the following day. Summer allows itself to die, dropping its leaves and seeds, so that as winter takes over it gives enough rain for the leaves to turn to nourishing soil, and it gives the seeds enough time to germinate in that soil.

Summer and winter, Life and Death, and the worlds above and below are all symbolised by light and dark deities such as Zeus, king and god of the Sky, and Hades, king and god of the Underworld. As Zeus's dark reflection, Hades was sometimes referred to as "Zeus Cthonos", Subterranean Zeus. In part, Zeus's origins lie with the sky god that tribes such as the Dorians brought into Greece from the North, but his other aspect comes from the ancient Bronze Age culture in Minoan Crete. Here he was believed to have been born in one cave, and to have died in another cave! In this way, his origins are connected to those of Dionysos, for this aspect of Zeus was a god who was born and died and was reborn with the seasons. He was the son-lover and consort of the great Mother Goddess. An early name for Dionysos was Dionysos Zagreus, and the name Zeus, "lighting up", is in part derived from the name Zagreus, "restored to life".

As with Dionysos, the serpent was also one of Zeus's symbols and in legend Zeus unites with Persephone (daughter of Zeus and the fertility goddess Demeter) in the form of a serpent. The child of their union, which is born in the Underworld after Hades has abducted Persephone, is Dionysos Zagreus. Dionysos was often linked to birth or rebirth in a cave, such as the Corycian Cave near Delphi, while it was also a belief that Apollo was born in the darkness of a cave, despite his connection to the sun. The miracle of rebirth in the Underworld is the key. The forces of Light and Dark are intertwined like the serpents on the caduceus, the rod that belonged to the god Hermes, as psychopompos a traveller between the worlds of Illumination and Darkness.

In *The Goddess Within,* J.B. Woolger and R.J. Woolger say of Persephone that it is Zeus' dark brother Hades who saves her. It is the soul in the depths, the painful encounter with Hades that enables her to grow and flourish in a new way. Initiation occurs in the Subterranean Realm, as does the renewal of Life underground in the winter. However, life cannot bloom without the summer. The myth tells that after Persephone's abduction, only winter exists while Demeter mourns, until Persephone is returned to her for the summer months, thus creating a seasonal balance.

An even more ancient myth of a similar nature comes from Sumeria. Here it is a dark goddess of Death, Ereshkigal, who rules the Underworld, and her sister the bright goddess of Life, Inanna, who rules the Upper world. Inanna descends into the Underworld willingly, because she has a deep knowledge that she depends on Ereshkigal for her own death and resurrection. For the Sumerians this myth also symbolised the changing seasons and the cyclic powers of renewal. The terrifying dark goddess of death held the key to the creation of new life.

Another dark goddess is the Indian Kali, most often depicted as a death goddess, adorned with and surrounded by symbols of death and destruction. Yet, as Joseph Campbell points out, her right side gestures are "fear not" and "bestowal of boons". Within her destructive energy is paradoxically the gift of Life. Jean Houston compares Kali with the ancient Greek snake-haired Gorgon Medusa, who in mythology turns men to stone with one stare. Medusa is depicted on the shield of the goddess Athena, for the bright goddess holds the dark one as part of herself. Medusa is the wild and destructive side that Athena controls and contains. Athena is cultured and wise, but she is also a warrior, and therefore requires an element of destructive energy. Even the intuition that feeds her wisdom, and the inspiration that nourishes her cultural and musical abilities, as with Apollo, have a deep connection with the darkness below, for they rise from the subconscious. Houston says, "For me Medusa is also an emblem of my belief that in our most fearsome and loathsome quality lies the basis of our most creative luminous expression." Herein once again lies the mystery of the paradoxical nature of the Dark Twin/Brother/Sister energy.

Since the time of the ancient Greeks, the Greek goddess Hecate has been seen as an evil queen of witches. This is an unfortunate distortion of her nature. As the dark aspect of the Triple moon goddess of Maiden (Kore), Mother (Demeter) and Crone (Hecate), she is a necessary force. As with Kali as a bestower of boons and with Hades in his "Plutos" ("wealth") aspect, Hecate not only has the power to take things away from us, but she is also the giver of gifts. From underground come treasures, precious stones, gold and silver, and if we dig deep into our subconscious, we release our priceless gift of inspiration. In Hecate's role as Crone, however, she stands for what we often most fear losing. We do not relish the prospect of losing our youth, we dread the loss through death of those we love, and we fear our own deaths. However, with age comes the gift of deep wisdom, if we are willing to key into it. It is what C.G. Jung referred to as "individuation". This occurs when we are finally able to assimilate a lifetime's experience with a strong connection to our inner world. With death comes the great mystery of the eternal beyond, where all our souls nourish the over-soul, of which we are a part, and where various forms of rebirth are possible. Hecate also stands at the Crossroads, wherever transitions or difficult life decisions need to be made. Here again, we need to intuit and receive her wisdom, instead of giving in to our fear. Then we feel confidence in our choice and we embrace the challenge of a new, untrodden road. Hecate's symbol is the key. Because she holds the key to the gates of change at the crossroads of life, she presides over the transitions between all the aspects of the Triple Goddess, of which she is a part. She opens the portals between youth and maturity, maturity and old age, old age and death, and death and rebirth. She unites Light and Dark aspects in the cycle of Life.

The dark cthonic gods, goddesses and deities have existed in various forms for many thousands of years, because they are an essential part of us, as well as our surroundings. Their terrifying aspects warn us against losing control of our negative traits. However, in leading us through the depths to our intuitive and creative source, they open what William Blake referred to as the doors of perception. They enable us to face and negotiate the awkward transitions, and they finally initiate us into the great mystery of transformation. They contain within their being an element of the opposite energy, their Light counterparts. Later in this book, the "parallel universe" of the dark realm of the subconscious is explored as a mirror reflection of the light realm of consciousness, and visa versa. It is part of the paradox of life that opposite forces have much in common with each other! Each apparently incompatible personality is a complementary counterpart to its opposite.

M. Rilke once described death as the side of life averted from us. The dark power is part of one force, for it is the dark side of the illuminating Spirit of Life. Ultimately, they are one.

The Black Sheep

# THE BLACK SHEEP

*When a true genius appears in the world, you may know him by*
*this sign that the dunces are all in confederacy against him.*
Jonathan Swift, 1739

Whenever anyone feels different or out of place in a situation, that person knows what it feels like to be the "odd one out" or the "Black Sheep". The more often one finds oneself in this position, the more of the Black Sheep one is, and the more one feels shunned and undervalued.

People have a tendency to fear any situation or person that appears to threaten or undermine the status quo or the stability of the group. They are afraid of insecurity and the risk of change. Moreover, many that persecute those who do not fit in are actually shunning the Black Sheep within themselves. All aspects of the Dark Twin reside within the unconscious of everyone, but some of these traits like the Black Sheep tend to be suppressed, due to the desire and the pressure to conform and because of the terror of being ostracised. People usually want to be an accepted and respected part of society and are therefore fearful of any influence that could awaken and activate the Black Sheep within.

If we can put our fears and prejudices to one side, we open ourselves up to recognising our unique gift of ingenuity that is held within the folds of the Black Sheep's cloak. As the Black Sheep is an essential part of the Dark Twin, the gift is also from that inner sibling. It therefore possesses great power, for as Joseph Campbell says in *The Power of Myth*, "What's running the show is what's coming up from way down below."

On the surface, it appears to be a contradiction that given the prejudice against the Black Sheep, he or she can actually be in control. The influence of the moon provides an analogy. As there are thirteen phases of the moon each year, thirteen is the moon's magic number. Western society believes that number to be unlucky, accentuates the negative influence of the full moon, from which we have the word "lunatic", and denigrates the ancient moon goddess Hecate as an evil witch. It follows the masculine solar Apolline values of success, material achievement and spiritual and moral conformity, while devaluing the lunar cyclical and feminine traits. However, the undercurrents of life have their own rules. The moon's gravitational pull creates the tides, and as we consist of at least 70% water, we are affected too. We are aware that a full moon affects us, for our moods are heightened at this time, not just for the worse but also for the better, depending on our state of mind. It does affect our moods and rhythms at all times, for we tend to be more extroverted during the waxing, but more introverted during the waning, with the seeds of new ideas being planted at the time of a new moon. The moon's subliminal influence is much stronger than we realise.

The Black Sheep operates as a subliminal but powerful force, despite being devalued and unacknowledged so often. As with other gifts of the Dark Twin, that of the Black Sheep guards against stagnation and complacency. It enables a person to be a catalyst for change or creative inspiration. One musician, who has an imaginative and inventive approach to his music, was once in a band that had an original musical sound with a magical atmosphere. Other band members tended to underestimate his contribution, and he felt like the undervalued black sheep. However, once he had left the band, their sound remained competent and actually became more commercial, but the creative innovation and the essential sparkle had diminished. However, the musician retained it in his work. As an undercurrent force, he had played a strong part in "running the show".

Sometimes the powerful influence of the Black Sheep does not reveal itself until a later point in time. For instance, Galileo was regarded as a threat and a heretic in his own time for proclaiming the earth to be round, but he paved the way for others to explore the patterns of the solar system and to reveal the truth. Van Gogh's work initiated the Expressionist movement in the world of art, but at the point he died as a broken man who felt out of step with the world, he was little appreciated.

The immensely powerful undercurrents created by the Black Sheep can often work like a tsunami. Invariably, the wave is barely noticeable as it travels underneath the surface of the ocean, but as the land rises beneath, the wave suddenly builds, often to a great height, and floods the land with gigantic force. This phenomenon can occur with a group of people, as much as with individuals.

The blacks of the United States are an example of the Black Sheep taking on the form of a group. From the moment they were brought over as slaves, their culture and colour was derided. Although the situation did gradually improve, it was still bad well into the twentieth century and a lot of the prejudice still exists today. Sammy Davis Jnr. commented that being a star enabled him to be insulted in places where the average black person could never hope to be insulted. Between themselves they kept the soul of their culture very much alive, and in the sixties it burst through to the surface as a strong Black movement. The power of their music exemplified this phenomenon. The Black sound of the Blues was now upheld and developed by blacks such as Howling Wolf and Jimi Hendrix, and was taken on by whites like the Rolling Stones and Eric Clapton. It was now the driving force of the music scene and an integral part of the culture that accompanied it. The Black tsunami had surfaced! The

Black Sheep can have such a positive and powerful influence that it crashes through the barriers and bonds of prejudice and conventionality.

Despite the successful examples, there are times when the force of those who hold the reigns of power and who have the upper hand is so repressive and abusive that it turns the Black Sheep into the monster that he or she is accused of being. We see this syndrome in famous classics. In Emily Brontë's book *Wuthering Heights*, Heathcliff is the Black Sheep, shunned by the autocratic Hindley. Heathcliff's love for Hindley's sister Cathy, which is genuine and intense, has the potential to liberate Cathy from a monotonous existence dominated by polite society and material values. However, Cathy's confusion and Hindley's cruelty, as well as the rejecting society, turn Heathcliff into a vengeful, embittered "monster", who eventually brings misery to all he becomes involved with. Likewise, Frankenstein's "monster" creation in Mary Shelley's book shows the potential for good in the way he supports the blind girl, who is the only person to sympathise with him. However, he is turned into the very dangerous beast society and his maker believe him to be, due to their destructively negative reaction to his odd appearance. Real life reveals the same patterns. For instance, a ten-year-old girl who came from the north of England started at a school in the south and was immediately shunned by the rest of the class because of her different accent. She was intelligent, good natured and artistic, but the more she was abused by her classmates, the more embittered she became, and eventually that was all she was able to express. As Brian Keenan wrote in his book *An Evil Cradling,* "We become our meaningful selves only if people receive meaning from us."

It takes a lot of strength, courage and self-knowledge to stand up to rejection and heavy antagonism. Some people force themselves to conform in order to avoid the problem, but then become repressed and are unable to be themselves. Black sheep have to fight the internal enemy of self-doubt and low self-esteem, upon which the outer "enemy" of prejudice feeds, in order to avoid becoming like either a sadistic monster or a masochistic cripple.

With strength and encouragement, it is possible for the Black Sheep to reveal the positive potential, even if he or she has been pulled down the destructive path.

> That which hitherto has been a threatening or destructive entity can become co-operative and reveal its constructive potential when we risk finding a place for it and when we seek its inmost core of meaning.
> E.C. Whitmont, *The Symbolic Quest*

A story expressing this phenomenon is the fairytale *Beauty and the Beast.* The genuine love that Beauty develops for the Beast eventually turns him back into the handsome prince he once was. This story shows the need for the Black Sheep to reveal the hidden magical gift, and how important it is for that gift to be recognised. There is a need for others to appreciate the potential of the Black Sheep, however unattractive or strange the personality might appear to be. Many Black Sheep develop their negative tendencies due to trauma or rejection in childhood. It is only a small percentage of people who are so severely damaged that they are irredeemable.

Black Sheep can be the mentally ill, who have in the past been locked away in "lunatic asylums" and labelled as "possessed" or "beyond help". However, as the psychoanalyst R.D. Laing observed, breakdown could become breakthrough. Some patients of his, such as Mary Barnes who recovered enough to make a positive contribution to society, showed that this was possible. Laing said that although mystics and schizophrenics enter the same ocean, the mystics swim, while the schizophrenics drown. He recognised the potential gift held within the mind of the schizophrenic. Indeed, a number of the shamans of tribal groups are believed to have been schizophrenic, but far from being shunned or repressed by society, they were given the space to work through their illness to release their potential. Through the gifts of creativity, healing, and a psychic link to the spirit world, they became powerful aids to their communities.

The plights of Vincent Van Gogh and Jimi Hendrix show the fine divide between insanity and genius, and the importance of recognising the latter in a person. Van Gogh's mental illness finally overcame him, for he felt misunderstood and unappreciated. Hendrix was marginalised because of both his colour and his innovative eccentricity. However, once he was recognised in the UK and Europe, he was then accepted by his homeland. People are afraid of that which is different, yet they are also impressed by the success of something new or innovative. The Black Sheep can suddenly become a popular eccentric, or even an idol, if one area of the establishment has been prepared to overlook its prejudice and take a risk. Hendrix was not able to contain his self-destructive side in the last analysis, but he was able to show the world how bright the flame of genius can burn. His music crashed through existing boundaries and he was a creative example and inspiration to many.

In order to release the gift, the Black Sheep has to find the right niche. Sometimes, as in Hans Christian Anderson's fairytale *The Ugly Duckling*, a person is a Black Sheep because of not having found his or her own kind. Having friends who share interests and who can often become "soul-mates" provides a sense of well being. Once a Black Sheep feels invalidated in this way, he or she is more able to cope with the world and to shine. Invariably, there is also another aspect to the "odd one out" syndrome. Having a child in the family or a person in a group who is "different" is what is required to avoid stagnation within that collection of people. As with the story of the musician, while the Black Sheep is part of the group, perspectives are broadened.

The Black Sheep is an envoy of change and development. He or she is the unwanted but deeply needed gift, and has arrived to break the mould to enable movement to take place. Given the chance, the Black Sheep broadens and enriches the perspectives and lives of others. The one who initially seems and feels like an oddity or a "freak" is invariably a bright beacon of light in disguise, like the beast that turns into a handsome prince, or the ugly duckling that transforms into a beautiful swan. The Black Sheep transforms into a shining Krishna-like figure that illuminates a new path as the Piper who leads the dance.

The Trickster

# THE TRICKSTER

*He is both subhuman and superhuman, a bestial and divine being...*
C.G. Jung

There never was a "Once upon a time" in Trickster's story, because he has always been in existence. In the dawn of time he detonated the charge of the Big Bang. He danced amidst the volatile firmament, hurling balls of fire in all directions, and stirring luminous gasses with his twirling feet.

Trickster involved himself with both the conception and birth of Gaia, Mother Earth. Along with various spirits of creation, harmony and destruction, Trickster accompanied Gaia throughout her childhood, informing her of the advantage of his ways. After a time, she began to give birth to innumerable children. He worked with her to aid the survival of all the offspring she was creating and supporting, so both aggressors and potential prey alike would stand a better chance with the aid of Trickster's ingenious mantle of camouflage.

However, Trickster was not to be trusted. Exerting his influence, he encouraged some of Gaia's offspring to grow so greedy and powerful that they threatened the lives of far too many smaller children. Knowing it was Trickster's job to resolve the problem he had created, Gaia called on him to summon the gods of chaos and destruction over which he had control to oust and obliterate the aggressors. This Trickster agreed to do with pleasure, as earth shattering events were even more appealing to him than his violent monster friends, and the path was now cleared for the little creatures he had spared to one day grow to be even more powerful...

Gaia realised the trouble making nature of Trickster, but she needed him. With his cunning, he helped her to create increasingly intelligent children, who developed better chances of survival through learning some of the secrets of Trickster's ways. When Gaia finally gave birth to the human race, Trickster rubbed his hands with glee. Humans were particularly fun and interesting to play with, to use, and to teach.

Gaia grew increasingly uneasy as Trickster became closely involved with these creatures, helping them to develop such powerful forces that they finally reached the brink of disaster, when their greed and their dangerous inventions and actions threatened the lives of nearly all her children, including themselves!

This is the point our story has reached. Fond as she is of these creatures, Gaia has cried out to them to turn away from destruction. Trickster is watching closely. He is in a dilemma. He does not wish to lose his favourite playmates, and he could do more to encourage their amazing potential for creative expression. Yet Armagedon would be such an exciting experience, and it would clear the way for a whole host of new creations...

\* \* \* \* \* \* \*

C.G. Jung believed the trickster to be a universal shadow that was a parallel of the individual shadow. As a spirit who exists both inside us and around us at all times, he is ready to leap into action in accordance with his nature when we least expect him to. As a universal shadow, in essence he is what we do not want to see as part of our lives. He is the art of deception, a dangerous liar, the unpredictable, the joker and fool, and destruction and chaos. His presence makes us feel uncomfortable and insecure.

The trickster's character traits reveal themselves in many ways, as Jung says, ranging from the bestial to the divine. In his deceptive role, he can be mischievous and childlike, as with the practical joker antics of Puck in *A Midsummer Night's Dream*. He can be thoroughly evil, for instance, as the Norse trickster god Loki, who allows jealousy to lead him to trick the blind god Hod into killing the god Balder. Real life can also expose the evil aspect of the trickster, as with the Nazis, when they tricked the Jews into believing they were on their way to a new community. The Nazis asked everyone to pack all their possessions, which the people would never need for themselves in the concentration camps they were about to be sent to. The Roman senators tricked Julius Caesar into believing that he had their support, so he would voluntarily walk into the trap of their plan to murder him.

> And oftentimes, to win us to our harm,
> The instruments of darkness tell us truths,
> Win us with honest trifles, to betray's
> In deepest consequence.
> Shakespeare, *Macbeth*

The trickster is thoroughly resourceful. Besides childish trickery and evil trickery, there is that used for survival. Those who hid the Jews to spare them from the concentration camps had to trick the authorities into believing there were no extra people in their homes. In the fairytale *Hansel and Gretel*, Hansel puts a bone through his cage for the witch to feel instead of his finger, to make the half blind witch believe that he is not fat enough to eat. Odysseus is an example of a mythical trickster hero whose survival often depends on his trickster intelligence. He tricks both the Cyclops and the Sirens, in order to escape their murderous intent. He also employs a more insidious form of trickery, for it is his idea to create the Trojan horse, which carries Greek soldiers and which tricks the Trojans into believing it to be a peace offering. The ancient Greeks were proud of their inheritance and used Odysseus' story to exemplify the superiority of the intelligence they believed had brought greatness to their civilisation. Originally, Poseidon was not just the Sea God, for he was god of the Earth itself. His symbol was a horse. When archaeologists excavated Troy they discovered that in the era the war supposedly occurred, an earthquake and an armed raid destroyed the city. In his book *In Search of the Trojan War*, Michael Wood suggests that a wooden effigy of a horse may have been built by the Greeks to thank Poseidon for letting them in with his earthquake. He thinks that years later the story was changed to one of ingenious trickery, because of the belief that cunning intelligence was a virtue fit for a hero and the civilisation he helped create.

The trickster's ways can be used to promote peace, harmony and understanding. There is an old African story, which tells of two men who argue and fight over whether a man who passed by wore a black or a white hat. Finally, the man with the hat laughs and shows them that it is black on one side, but white on the other. This kind of trickery reveals the stupidity and potentially dangerous nature of a refusal to see beyond the obvious, and it also shows that there is often another side to an argument. The two men in the story learn this lesson, and are forever after the best of friends.

When we find ourselves in a bad situation, the trickster can play a positive role as our sense of humour, enabling us to temporarily imagine that we are not suffering. This helps us to hold on to the strength that we need to fight any feelings of hopelessness, which can threaten to overwhelm us. In the guise of jester, the trickster also points out truths that could be too dangerous or painful if delivered in a serious manner. By appearing to joke and make fun, the Fool in Shakespeare's *King*

*Lear* is the only character who can usually in court speak the truth without being condemned for it. Exposed to the wild elements on the heath, which brings the Fool into his own element, he is able to lead Lear to realise the folly of his pride. It is only through a growing state of insanity and the influence of the Fool that Lear's eyes are opened to the truth.

The trickster's games work not just through individuals, but through life's situations, as if the trickster spirit himself is moving people and elemental forces around in a complex game of chess. Here again his role is often that of a teacher or guide through his domain of the chaotic, bizarre or difficult situation.

On one occasion, during the filming of a short drama, conditions were so hazardous that the weatherman on television advised people not to go out. The filming had to go ahead anyway, as there was a tight budget and fifty people were lined up to work that night. However, half way through the night one of the principal actors refused to do his last scene, because it was on a windswept bridge, where it was indeed dangerous, with the odd light exploding as it crashed to the ground! But this was a major problem for the director to deal with, because it was the final and most important scene in the film. With the cameraman, she had to work out a completely alternative ending there and then on the spot. What transpired to be particularly interesting was that the newly invented scene created in a hurry under extreme duress turned out to be a far more powerful scene than the one the writer/director had spent hours painstakingly working out! It could be construed that this odd twist in events had the trickster spirit behind it!

Another strange true-life experience occurred when, as a student in London, I had arranged to meet my mother at Victoria Station. Due to tension and exhaustion on that day I fell asleep, and was consequently an hour late for the rendezvous! When I arrived at the station, I could not see my mother. Thoroughly anxious, I was about to ask if a message could be given over the loud speaker, when a train pulled in and my mother appeared. The train was an hour late! It was very unusual for me to be that late, and trains do not often run behind to that degree. The rest of the evening followed a similar pattern of things apparently going seriously wrong, but then miraculously resolving themselves. Perhaps the trickster spirit was playing games in order to show the two of us that we could have some faith in the flow of life's events without panicking if any given situation appeared to be spinning out of control.

A peculiar real-life story of a serious nature happened to a woman who had married a violent man with a terrible temper. He always struck fear into others. The only thing he really feared was the thought of ever having a handicapped child. They subsequently had a son, who was severely ill when he was still a baby. He survived, but from that time on he was partially paralysed and had suffered brain damage. However, the father who had always dreaded such a situation, became extremely caring with the child, and went through a total personality change. From that point onwards he was a gentle, balanced character. Fortunately too, the child had a bright, sunny personality, and as he grew up he was consequently able to cope better with his disability than others might have been. The trickster spirit might well have been at work here, presiding as he does over strange twists of fate.

The paradoxical or bizarre situation is the trickster's domain. To carry his purpose through, he sometimes goes beyond mere trickery to the instigation of change and chaos. In this sense he is a Dionysian force. Change often creates turmoil and upsets the balance of life, but not without reason. As Plato wrote, "When the mood of the music changes, the walls of the city shake." Without the trickster's winds of change, the music of life would become monotonously repetitive and the city would lose its vitality and become tired, lifeless and frustrated. William Blake expressed this sentiment when he wrote, "The man who never alters his opinion is like standing water, and breeds reptiles of the mind." Shamans around the world have generally taken on the trickster's mantle, for in addition to various roles, including that of taking the lead in passed down ritual, they serve as promoters of fresh creativity and change through their dreams and inner inspiration. The North American Indians revered their trickster god Coyote (the fox), because they realised that breaking taboos and stirring up chaos was an intrinsic part of life, for without that force, stagnation would set in.

The trickster is the unpredictable conjurer. As the shape-changing creator of spells in his role of Magician or Wizard, to coin the phrase used by Tom Chetwynd in his *Dictionary of Symbols*, the trickster is "the Lord of Phantasmagoria". In this guise he is an inspiration for the creative imagination. He moves between the conscious and unconscious mind, acting as a bridge between the two. Artists, musicians, poets, storytellers, actors or filmmakers, all trick the mind into seeing the world of imagination as a reality. Yet, who is to say what reality really is? Our inner world is what drives our hearts and our spirits, and it is what gives meaning, colour and light to all we see and feel. Through the power of our imagination we unlock the door to that place, which is an infinite universe where we can constantly expand our horizons beyond the safe and the known. It is what Brian Keenan refers to as "this unexplored landscape".

As in the Trickster and Gaia story at the beginning of this chapter, the trickster is a playful character. He is highly dangerous if unchecked and separated from the force that regulates Life's patterns, because he is a hedonist and on his own he has no moral code, but he is vital for the development and continuation of life. It is the trickster's job to ignite our imagination and to play games with our lives, tripping up the apparent harmony when it is time for our horizons to broaden and when stagnation threatens to set in. If we dance alone with the trickster for too long, we lose our equilibrium and we risk bringing about violent self-destruction. However, if we defy the trickster, a meaningless wasteland builds in our hearts and our creative life force becomes blocked like a dammed up river. As a supportive agent of Life and Mother Earth, and therefore a positive aspect of the Dark Twin, the trickster performs a vital role. If mankind can learn to be less power seeking, greedy and short sighted, the trickster will be an inspiration, revealing an increasing amount of his magic, which opens the door to the boundless ocean of our spirit. Unfortunately, the more greed there is in the world, the more the destructive, negative traits of the trickster come into play, and like the Pied Piper with the rats, he could eventually lead us over the edge of the precipice we have created. The choice is in our hands; it is up to us.

The Dark Force in Nature

# THE DARK FORCE IN NATURE

> Nature, like the Sphinx, is of womanly celestial loveliness and tenderness, the face and bosom of a goddess, but ending in claws and the body of a lioness. There is in her celestial beauty... but there is also a darkness, ferocity, fatality which are infernal. She is a goddess, but one not yet disimprisoned - the articulate, lovely, still encased in the inarticulate, chaotic. How true! And does she not propound her riddles to us?
> Thomas Carlyle

How deep and how ancient is the infernal aspect of the Dark Twin? We can all point to hideous deeds committed by mankind, but did "evil" exist before man ever emerged? Nature itself, as the Sphinx reveals, is indeed a paradox that encompasses darkness and destruction, but is this aspect what we would term as "evil"?

"Thou Nature art my goddess" are the opening lines of Edmund in Shakespeare's *King Lear*. Edmund is an evil human predator, unhampered by conscience. He believes that because of his illegitimacy he has no allegiance to law and order, and therefore can happily follow the rule of "survival of the fittest", trickery and savage killing. As Edmund observes, all of these traits can be seen in nature. However, hatred and a desire for revenge drive Edmund. The animal predator kills to survive. In Farley Mowat's book *Never Cry Wolf,* he explains how he was sent to the Yukon wastelands to find out why wolves were killing more and more caribou. He discovered that man was indiscriminately shooting the fit, strong caribou, so the herd was getting increasingly weaker. The wolves only went for the weak ones, so were now killing more. Man had upset the balance.

In William Golding's *Lord of the Flies*, young boys stranded on an island revert to a savage, destructive state. The island, which is untamed and wild, appears to be the catalyst for the breakdown of the boys' social behaviour. These are boys with a rigid, strict background; they are public school boys. So the release from the repressed ordered world is a swing to the opposing force of anarchy, out of which the public school bully and predator hunter Jack forms a new hierarchy. So, is it really the influence of raw nature itself that is "evil", or is it that the wild exposes the truth of a life of organised repression and the values of power, intimidation and control?

In the ancient Greek myth of King Pentheus of Thebes, Pentheus believes in the omnipotence of social order and rigid laws. He therefore refuses to acknowledge the anarchic nature god Dionysos. In revenge, Dionysos drives the women of the town mad and Pentheus' own mother kills him. The balance of nature is upset when repression leads to an explosive reaction. Everything polarises and evil is the result. It has the same effect as when a volcano violently explodes because the pressure has built up to an extreme degree under a strong volcanic plug.

"The horror, the horror!" cries the dying Kurtz in Joseph Conrad's *Heart of Darkness*. The jungle reflects back to Kurtz the horror of the tyrant that he has become. "We are accustomed to look upon the shackled form of a conquered monster, but there – there you could look at a thing monstrous and free" writes Conrad. He can see that nature in its wild state reflects and brings out the true nature of those who enter its domain, thus freeing up and playing upon any demons that might inhabit their inner selves.

To be exposed to the wildness of nature can be a terrifying experience. I had a strong sensation of this on a trip to India, where the force of Death was always close at hand, but where the vivid force of Life as his consort was equally powerful. India attacked my senses with its raw savage honesty. My vulnerability sometimes turned to terror, particularly one night when I dreamed a man was suffocating me and I awoke to find I was doing this to myself with curtains from the window behind! I felt the hot breath of the predator close behind at every turn. Yet, I also felt a strong pulse. Nothing could compare with the spiritual stillness of the Rhajasthan desert, or the purity and heavenly beauty of the rising sun blessing Mother Ganges with a rich golden light, while worshippers bathed in the incandescent waters. Then a shrouded figure would appear in the current, and a white limb poking out through the material would reveal this to be a dead body. The cold reality of death was exposed here. The spirit of this place was a powerful example of the paradox of the Sphinx, and the impact of the natural cycle unmasked.

Raw nature surrounding us is a way to lead us to the core of our own inner nature, the realm of the Dark Twin. That is why shamans and mystics have ventured to the wilderness, whether it be heath-land, mountains, jungle, frozen wasteland or desert, to be initiated. It is in these places that the innermost truth can be faced. This can be savagely dangerous for the unprepared, as in the Arthurian story when the knights who venture into the wild lands fail to find the grail and die, or in tribal stories of potential shamans who are either wounded or killed because they do not pass the test. Here we meet the paradoxical experience of the Mexican Huichol tribe referred to in the first chapter, and we know we are in the presence of the Dark Twin. Those with sufficient strength and purity of heart are transformed with the harsh and ecstatic experience of spiritual death and rebirth.

So, nature brings out the true nature that lies within our hearts, whether it is good, bad, courageous or fearful.

If it is positive and centred, we are often given heightened powers, as with the shamans, Jesus or Buddha. If it is either bad or fearful, it appears that nature mirrors and reacts to the imbalance within us in a destructive manner. Nature becomes negative whenever the equilibrium is upset.

Lyall Watson comments in his book *Dark Nature* that nature itself has no morals as such, but that it does follow the Goldilocks theory put forward by the scientific writer John Gribbin, which is the pull towards the situation that is in balance. That does not mean a move towards a permanent state of harmony, because there is also a need for the trickster, the chaos factor that avoids stagnation. Chaos and harmony, flux and flow, and the cycles of death and rebirth are all part of nature's pattern, for in this way, life changes, evolves and develops. Nature can be brutally cruel and uncaring, yet it also gives birth and nurtures, and it is always working towards equilibrium. The two forces of positive and negative are in constant interplay, each giving rise to the other and sometimes with extreme swings. As Nature incorporates the force of violent destruction, one could say that evil does exist in it, but as an unintentional trampling over life forms rather than greed or a desire to inflict cruelty. In this mode it is amoral rather than purposefully evil. Sometimes Nature's destruction is part of the aim towards the best possible chance for the survival of Life.

Nature does indeed present us with the paradox of the Sphinx. We are bound to also ponder on the confusing paradox of our own nature, with such a potential to create a beautiful world, and with the power of reasoning and conscience to enable us rise above brutality. Yet we are probably the most destructive creatures this planet has ever experienced. The Sphinx must have smiled when we were created!

The Dark Force in its
Constructive Role

# THE DARK FORCE IN ITS
# CONSTRUCTIVE ROLE

*Even as the stone of the fruit must break, that its heart may
stand in the sun, so must you know pain.*
Kahlil Gibran

   ·   Life, Death, Love, Anger, Creation, Destruction, Joy
and Pain are all states of being that can be seen as
characters in a story or players on a stage or in a film. The
"bad guy" has his part to play as much as the "good guy".
Whether it is the Hero, the Lover, the Friend, the
Trickster, or the Nemesis, each character contributes to
the story. There is often a happy ending, but a sacrifice
has invariably been made and the painful process of death
and rebirth has generally taken place. If there had been no
"spanner in the works", then the entertainment would have
been tedious and the audience or reader would have lost
interest or fallen asleep! We naturally recognise the need
for a challenging negative element to act as a catalyst for
movement, development and transformation.

Discomfort is found in the most natural of life's
occurrences. The birth experience is painful and traumatic
for both mother and child. Here again we experience
nature's paradox of pain and danger, yet at the same time
the wonder of life. The stories of the abduction of
Persephone by Hades, or the expulsion of Adam and Eve
from Eden are in part symbols for the pain of growing up,
with the loss of blissful innocence and the protection of
the parent. Pain and sacrifice accompany every stage of
growth and change.

Myth exposes another aspect of the paradox. The Gorgon Medusa turns men to stone with her gaze, but a drop of her blood can restore life. The poisonous belladonna deadly nightshade holds the key to a cure for cancer. The lethal venom from snakebite is also a curative medicine. In fact, the snake is the emblem for the medical profession and was the main symbol for the ancient Greek healer god Aesclepius. Every destructive thing in nature holds the key to its antidote. That is why it works to give a vaccination to people, for an injection of a small dose of a disease stops the disease itself from occurring.

Preventative measures may often appear "bad" or "cruel". When a parent disciplines a child by creating boundaries beyond which the child must not pass, it may seem harsh, but it prepares the child for social conduct. Nobody would want to know the child years later if he or she had been allowed to run riot!

If a situation is allowed to get worse, then a stronger dose of the counter negative is necessary. A sudden disturbing event can shake one out of a destructive groove. Chemotherapy is radical, but can cure cancer, and the Fire of London destroyed the plague. As Shakespeare puts it in *Hamlet*, "Diseases desperate grown, by desperate appliances are relieved or not at all."

The worse the situation, the more radical the cure. It can still work, but if it happens too late or in a dose that is too high, it can actually make the situation worse. It is a gamble and good judgement is needed.

Even our mistakes have a positive side, for they teach us if we are prepared to learn from them. It is the experience of life with all its complexities, which enables us to evolve, grow and develop. Risks are taken so that we can move forwards, and sacrifices are made for the good of the whole.

Pain, discord, discomfort, death and chaos can all be necessary and unavoidable. They are not essentially "evil" if they lead to the greater good. Negatives need to be recognised and addressed. We should acknowledge and shake hands with the dangerous gods like Hades, Greek god of the Dead, Kali, Hindu goddess of destruction, or Hecate, Greek goddess of dangerous choices and points of change. A small amount of their power is necessary, either to avoid stagnation so that life can move forwards, or in order to stop these forces from taking over. They only become "evil" if their energies are not harnessed and handled carefully. If they are denied, then too much light does indeed cast a very dark shadow and they burst forth in full fury, glory and horror. In fact, if any energy is denied, however "good" it is in itself, it can turn terrifyingly negative.

The Dark Force as
Pure Destruction

# THE DARK FORCE AS PURE DESTRUCTION

Life's but a walking shadow, a poor player
That struts and frets his hour upon the stage,
And then is heard no more; it is a tale told
By an idiot, full of sound and fury,
Signifying nothing.
William Shakespeare, *Macbeth*

Macbeth wades so deep into the mire of his evil deeds, that he eventually loses sight of the light of his own humanity. Blinded by this all-embracing darkness, life has lost its meaning. All he can feel waiting for him in the wings is an empty void. By this time, the only moment he feels alive is when he is going for the kill. His negativity has taken him over.

In his book *Dark Nature*, Lyall Watson talks of Bobby Thompson, who with another boy Jon Venables killed the small child James Bulger. Other than the obvious joy and satisfaction Thompson had experienced in the killing, Watson noticed while observing Thompson in the courtroom that his eyes expressed a chilling emptiness. The "occupant" was "out", and instead in his eyes was the "Other". It appeared that Thompson had become filled with a particular kind of emptiness, so that he only felt "alive" when being destructive.

The word "live" turned back to front spells "evil". Real evil is literally a negation of life. It is, however, not a passive void, because its ambition is to actively fulfil "The Nothing".

In Michael Ende's *The Never Ending Story*, a "Nothing" is gradually taking over a wonderful place called Fantastica, the world of the imagination. The greed of the Nothing knows no limits. Its appetite will never be satiated until it has completely swallowed all that exists. It operates like a black hole, a dark cold mass that sucks in living matter like a vacuum cleaner, or in the way the legendary vampire sucks the life-blood of his victim.

The vampire may be fictional, but it does exist as a force that drives a number of people. Those who possess this energy have a draining affect on those around them. They are not necessarily 'bad' people, but they are extremely needful and demand a lot of others, while giving very little of themselves. The vampire force can also exist within an individual like an internal parasite. In this case it is most likely to only harm the person concerned and those who care about the well being of that person.

The Dark Force, or Nothing, does affect everybody to a greater or lesser degree and in different ways. On the other hand, there do appear to be very few people in this world who have been totally taken over by it. Apparently, even Hitler was a vegetarian and loved animals! However, as in the case of Hitler, if it gains enough control to use someone as an active agent, playing on his or her potentially negative tendencies, such as envy, resentment or an obsessive ambition, it becomes increasingly harmful. It can also drive groups of people such as violent street gangs, or even whole nations, when they torture and destroy in their desire for control.

The only positive aspect of the Nothing is in the warning it gives. When people recognise it, they fight ever more strongly for love and life. Even this darkest force has its function, because our very fight against it makes us stronger. There is a saying, "That which does not kill you gives you strength". However, it is by far the best solution to quell this dark monster within each of us long before it is ever able to use us to invade or infect another. It is the one aspect of the Dark Twin that we need to actively defy and eradicate with our positive energy.

How Evil is Born

# HOW EVIL IS BORN

And out of good still to find means of evil.
John Milton, *Paradise Lost*

We are all sensitive instruments, for it is hard to stay in tune. We can easily be tipped off balance and we are always walking the tight rope. It is much more difficult to regain our equilibrium than to lose it further. Small problems snowball, from early mistakes and unmet needs to later violence and angst. A lot of negativity can be traced back through generations, for it is in many cases a domino effect. But the most problematical question is "What are the original causes?"

In his book, *Yin and Yang,* J. C. Cooper suggests that Shiva's dance turns from creation to destruction when he dances alone instead of with a woman, because there is no longer a balance. Any heavy emphasis on one thing to the exclusion of another is a strong root cause, whether it is denial, repression or excess! Even too much "good" can be our downfall! If we ignore the flow of the river or the course of Nature, and if we deny the existence and need for a small dose of chaos or pain, or even for excitement, all these things build behind the dam of our creation. When the pressure gets too great, they come rushing through in a violently destructive torrent. It is Nature's design for every deity to be involved with the process of life. In his book *Howards End*, E.M. Forster talks of how the Monk in us can deny the Beast to such a degree that the Beast threatens to take over. R.L. Stevenson's story *Dr. Jekyll and Mr. Hyde* reveals a similar polarity, for the polite and good mannered Dr. Jekyll turns into the savage

Mr. Hyde. The Shadow that Jung speaks of is the Dark Thing that is created from either negative feelings or purely natural drives we are ashamed of, and which we have pushed down underground.

We literally create demons. We give birth to forces that were originally normal drives. The sex drive can give joy and bond two people in an act of creation, whether literally or as inspiration. However, when it is repressed or denied, it can become dark and twisted and can lead to acts of violent aggression. As a child, my mother suffered in a convent school at the hands of nuns. The Mother Superior threatened to set her dog on girls who "misbehaved", and my mother was actually knocked out by another nun! By no means are all nuns that way inclined, but it shows that the syndrome can occur. Attitudes against any form of sexuality that did not comply with the narrow confines of social acceptability, as well as alternative beliefs or the more unconventional aspects of human behaviour and female wisdom, over the centuries have led to extreme cruelty. Religious groups and those in power have carried out many executions due to intolerance that continued from the end of the Roman era through to the eighteenth century.

Another form of evil is that of inflated self-importance. In Christian and Hebrew theology, evil is born when the angel Lucifer separates himself out from the other angels. It is again a "splitting off". This form of evil follows the same principle of denial, but in this case it is the rejection of the need for harmony and wholeness. The balance is upset by Lucifer's desire to stand out and set himself up on a pedestal.

If children are spoilt, they often grow up feeling in their self-importance that the world exists to serve them. On the other hand, abused children can grow up either harbouring a grudge, or else feeling that they owe the world a favour. These are examples of situations that reveal the genesis of an imbalance, but there are many other permutations. Problems can begin at any time in our lives, but children are particularly susceptible.

When an imbalance is created, need can easily turn to greed, admiration to jealousy, and low self-esteem to desperate ambition or a form of masochism. People can gradually turn into either persecutors or victims.

The internal invalidator can be equally as destructive as the outer one. For instance, addiction can create a living hell. The strange thing about addiction though is that as psychoanalyst M. Scott Peck says it is actually a quest for Eden, but the damage from the past has sent the person down the wrong path. Psychological damage can easily turn a potential genius into a ruined alcoholic.

It is a difficult task for all of us to fight our inner demons. Even if the worst ones are curbed, most people suffer to a greater or lesser degree from the demons of fear and laziness. The old saying attributed to Edmund Burke is "It is necessary only for the good man to do nothing for evil to triumph." The ostrich mentality often lets a bad situation get out of hand, and bullies are given free reign.

> For sweetest things turn sourest by their deeds;
> Lilies that fester smell far worse than weeds.
> Shakespeare, *Sonnet 94*

When anything festers, a chemical reaction takes place. Evil is the result of an unfortunate chemical reaction. All the ingredients are essentially neutral and are therefore in the first place a part of Nature's drive towards a state of equilibrium, as in the Goldilocks effect. Everything that has been tipped off balance was once a natural drive.

Our complexity as human beings means that it is very difficult for us to maintain our equilibrium, and as we are as paradoxical as Nature itself, we are perfect playthings for the Sphinx. We are able to choose to be moral, caring and social. With our powers of reasoning and compassion, we can decide to be vegetarian, to support the homeless or to help the starving in Africa. With our technology we can irrigate desert areas and we have made advanced discoveries in curing disease. Yet, we are the most destructive animals this planet has ever to our knowledge experienced, and we threaten the very survival of most living things, including ourselves. We have lives that are often divorced from the rhythm of nature, which means that the balance gets tipped very easily. Each time this happens, more "evil" is created, whether it is crime, poverty, war, or the destruction of the planet, and the challenge to "get things right" is ever harder to face. Humanity itself now needs to be aware that the dark force it has given birth to needs to be faced and transformed before the balance is completely lost and destruction takes over.

George Harrison once said that a forest could only be green if every tree is green. In our outer lives, we need to do all we can to fight injustice and pain. However, before judging others, we should first each look into our own hearts, for the initial journey of transformation starts there. The essence of our problems lies deep within, and therefore so does the solution. There is no short cut or easy way.

Compassion

# COMPASSION

And there are those who have little and give it all. These are the
believers in life and the bounty of life, and their coffer is never empty.
Kahlil Gibran, *The Prophet*

Compassion is opposed to the selfish, destructive
aspect of the Dark Twin, but paradoxically, there is an
element of his spirit within the nature of compassion. It
can involve stepping off the beaten track and going against
normal behaviour patterns, or the "party line". The
empathic person can become the Black Sheep aspect of
the Dark Twin through defying the prejudice, bigotry and
racism that are rife in most cultures. As the film *Cry
Freedom* illustrates, the South African Donald Woods
became an outcast and therefore a black sheep through his
support for the oppressed.

Compassion brings together the twins of darkness
and light. It casts light on to all aspects of the underbelly
of life, thus building a bridge between ordinary life and
the dreaded or despised underworld. Compassion defies
fear. It not only leads some to risk their lives for others,
but it also links people to the worlds of crime and insanity.
The concern Elizabeth Fry had for prisoners in the
nineteenth century threw light on to their predicament and
led to an improvement in prison conditions. R.D. Laing
defied established ways of treating mentally ill patients
through his empathy with their needs and feelings. For
instance, he believed the use of electric shock therapy to
be both dangerous and lacking in awareness. Elizabeth
Kubler-Ross devoted much of her life to helping the
terminally ill and the understanding of death. Compassion

of this nature even throws light on the dark god Hades.

A lack of compassion can occur when the Dark Twin takes over, but it can also be caused by an avoidance of him. Denial of our own dark aspect or shadow brings about a false sense of moral superiority. This has often led to cold-blooded cruelty and persecution of anyone who does not fit the accepted social norm, such as unmarried pregnant women, homosexuals, foreigners, or those who do not follow the accepted religious faith. When a sense of justice prevents any harsh action, the excesses of cruelty are curbed, but without compassion the balance is lost and the rigidity of denial creates a spiritual desert. Then the repressed Dark Twin is in danger of bursting forth in his negative aspect like a torrent breaking through a dam.

The evidence of compassion is clear, but it is not so easy to understand its origin. A teacher once told his class a story of a man who was taken on a visit to Hell. There he saw a table laden with food, but everyone around the table had one hand tied behind his or her back, while the other hand held a spoon. These spoons were so long that it was impossible for them to get the food into their mouths, so as with Tantalus in Tartarus, they were constantly desperate for food their mouths could not quite reach. The man was then taken to Heaven. Initially to his surprise, here was the same set up as in Hell, with the food-laden table and the long spoons. He then realised the only difference was that each person was feeding the other, so in this way everybody was well fed and happy. It had not occurred to the people in Hell to do that!

The above story could be interpreted as pointing out the altruism and natural mutual concern that people should have, or alternatively it could be viewed as pure common sense! After all, businessmen, companies and corporations co-operate as much as they compete, with the "you scratch my back, I'll scratch yours" strategy. This is practical decision making, as part of our drive to find the best possible survival patterns.

The Darwinian theory is that we think selfishly in order to survive and evolve successfully. Even the care we show for the children of our relations, as well as our own, scientists describe as "the selfish gene", because we do not only put ourselves first for survival, but also the genes of our own family group. There is also the "us and them" behaviour pattern, the way in which people put their own tribe, nation or race before any other, sometimes with hostility towards outsiders.

So, what about true compassion? To a greater or lesser degree, most people exhibit classically selfish behaviour patterns, but there are other patterns that unlock the doors to a much more miraculous level of our existence. If we only wish to protect the interests of ourselves and the group to which we belong, then why, for instance, does a man risk his own life to save a stranger from drowning? Why are we driven by compassion to help a stray dog or a bird with a damaged wing? Why do we feel the need to help the starving? Why, going beyond humans, does a dolphin purposely save a man's life? None of these drives can have anything to do with direct self-interest. In the spirit of the Dark Twin, the desire to help another can be powerful. People can feel driven to perform acts of compassion either at risk to themselves, or in defiance of what is allowed or expected of them.

As altruistic behaviour appears to exist more in species with complex social situations, such as humans, primates, whales and dolphins, it could well have been brought about through cultural, rather than genetic patterns, as Lyall Watson in his book *Dark Nature* points out. But even if these motivations began as cultural, they must have sunk into our psyche enough by now to be a part of our basic make up. We are afraid of the dark from early childhood, whether we have ever personally been exposed to the wild where beasts roam around or not! It is likely that our highly developed social patterns, formed over many thousands of years, extended the protective, loving feelings we have always had for our young and our clan to include other human beings, other creatures, and even to plants and trees. Our complexity might have separated us from nature in one way, but it has also given us the potential to develop a conscious sense of ourselves as an integral part of it.

The anthropologist Richard Leakey, who has made invaluable discoveries about the pre-history of mankind and who has studied the social patterns of various contemporary tribal groups, believes that the search for our ancestors gives us hope. In the conclusion of his book *The Making of Mankind,* he writes that we should take on a global responsibility for all forms of life in the world. He has understood the significance of human compassion, and he challenges humanity to become more in tune with it.

We humans, with our advanced capacity for compassion, are equally the species on this earth that creates more damage than any other species, and that even potentially threatens life on Earth, as we know it. The very development in our brains and social systems that led to our sense of compassion, also led to our superiority complex and our alienation from nature itself! Again, we meet the paradox of the Dark Twin. The positive counterpart to our arrogant negativity, our compassion, could give rise to a miracle that would explain why the cosmic gamble in the creation of our dangerous existence was worth taking!

There is a fundamental desire in humanity to protect and embrace Life itself. It is the recognition that all of us and all other living things are segments of the Whole. Chief Seattle said "Man did not weave the web of life; he is merely a strand in it. Whatever he does to the web, he does to himself"... "Everything is connected." While appealing to any compassion White Man might still feel, Chief Seattle was also warning him of his self-interest when he said, "He treats his mother, the earth, and his father, the sky, as things to be bought, plundered, sold like sheep or bright beads. His appetite will devour the earth and leave behind only a desert".

Those who put short-term gain and personal profiteering first tend to denounce compassion and concern for the environment as impractical, weak and sentimental. However, it is becoming increasingly apparent that the destruction Chief Seattle foretold is highly likely, if self-interest continues to hold sway. Pollution is already causing major problems, there is now a hole in the ozone layer, the ice caps are melting due to global warming, and forests and arable land are fast turning into deserts. Mankind is becoming so short-sighted, self-centred and greedy that there is not even enough concern over what kind of a world one's own children or grandchildren will grow up into. Here, the obsessed and self involved side of the Dark Twin within, that can only lead humanity down the path of destruction, is at work and is dancing extremely close to the edge of the precipice. However, it is still not too late to play on his positive aspect and activate his powers of transformation. After all, as a rebellious black sheep, he fans the flames of any revolt against the wrongs of the world, and our gift of compassion for all living things is now more vitally needed than ever before.

If we open ourselves up and connect with the whole of mankind and all other life forms, we gain a deeper understanding of the life force and the part we have to play. The union transforms darkness into light. It is the ultimate embrace, for it is compassion as love personified and felt at the deepest level. At the end of the day, love is the driving force behind any act of true compassion. When we feel it running through our veins like a river of light, we are compelled to follow its call. We flow towards the sea of creation with the revelation that we are all connected as One. We are stardust. As we are all part of the Great Spirit of Life, our personal growth enables it to grow. The more we love, the closer we are to the heartbeat of that mystery and the more we enable it to reveal its positive potential.

Passion

# PASSION

If in your fear you would seek only love's peace and love's pleasure, then it is better for you that you cover your nakedness and pass out of love's threshing floor, into the seasonless world where you shall laugh, but not all your laughter, and weep, but not all your tears.
Kahlil Gibran, *The Prophet*

Compassion is a driving force of any kind of real love, but passion is also a component. The intensity of passion warms and lifts the spirit to a deep and powerful sense of connection with the beloved or object of love. Great artistic achievements that have given joy and insight to many have been driven by passion. Dante's *Divine Comedy* was inspired by his love for a woman, Beatrice. Emily Brontë's passion for the soul of the wild heath-land inspirited her *Wuthering Heights.* Passion moves people to perform acts that are beyond the normal level of existence. The strength of Lady Jane Franklin's love for her husband, Sir John Franklin, led her to continue the search for his lost ship in the North West Passage, long after others had given up, and it was due to her persistence that the mystery began to be resolved. Mahatma Gandhi's impassioned love of his oppressed fellow Indians led to his inspirational acts of bravery, as he devoted his life to striving for peace and freedom for India. Passion raises love to the transcendent and enables it to break through restricting established boundaries.

However, when passion is driven by negative feelings, a lot of harm can be done in the name of love. In *An Evil Cradling* Brian Keenan writes about how love can become confused with power. Observing the men who kept him hostage in Beirut, he recognised how civil unrest and the hardship of poverty could create the low self-esteem and frustration that lead to anger, violence and a burning desire for self-empowerment and domination. The symbol of power that becomes the apparent object of love can be anything, such as a dominating family, religion, or a political ideal.

Love loses its meaning when the lust for power takes over. The desire for having exclusive power over others is alienating and emotionally suffocating. Possessiveness that calls itself love restricts the spirit. The "love" of a country can develop into nationalism if the motivation is essentially prejudice against outsiders and a sense of innate superiority. In extreme cases this leads to war, as with Nazi Germany.

Without compassion, passion can easily turn negative. When the perverted, self-centred aspects of the Dark Twin eat into the heart, then love is distorted into a petrified mask that only masquerades as the truth it once was. The spirit of love has then lost its meaning. Even in personal relationships, the passionate intensity of feeling can lead to a loss of balance. If a parent is unable to keep the child in check, then the strong emotional bond can lead to exhaustion and frustration. In romantic love, if anything impedes or blocks the relationship, then passion can turn into an intense sadness or anger, ruthlessly killing the very essence of the inspiration it invoked. However, when the balancing influence of compassion is allowed to merge with the passion, the river of love is able to flow and a deep joy and sense of purpose spring up from within.

The paradoxical nature of passion and the depths from which it rises reveals it to be from the realm of the Dark Twin, where all the raw energies of the subconscious are tapped. The power of it moves people to transcend themselves and to risk their lives. It is one way of helping people to endure torture and hardship and to face their deepest fears. In romantic love, this is where both the wild ecstacy of Dionysos and the chilling darkness of Hades perform an exquisite, yet terrifying dance of Life and Death. Passion is the opened heart that invites pain as much as delight, and when driven by compassion, the heartache is embraced as much as the joy.

Creativity

# CREATIVITY

*He who is born in imagination discovers the latent forces of nature.*
Paracelsus

Many see creativity as sacred to artists, musicians, dancers, writers and poets. The god of creativity is worshipped and invoked by these people, but should not be seen as exclusively their domain. Everybody is creative in some way. There is an art to cooking, to choosing clothes, to homemaking, to gardening, to entertaining friends, to bringing up children, to working out a business plan or a new computer game. The magic of creativity works through many aspects of life, so this chapter is applicable to everyone. However, there are many levels of creativity. The source or essence of this phenomenon exists at the deepest levels, entered by those who are willing to tread the winding and stony pathways to the place where they can embrace the mystery of the creative process, in its many aspects.

C.G. Jung believed that in order to be able to think in an original way, and therefore to be creative, one needed to leave the straight path where people go along with the flow of events, and to instead find the back streets and alleys. I experienced this in one of a number of unusual dreams I had when I was going through a transition from a stable, but static, way of life to a more unpredictable one. I heard sublime music in a cathedral. I thought that the source of it was high up towards the spire. However, as I tried to approach the sound, it faded. It was an illusion. A voice told me that I had to leave and find my way back from the outside before I could understand the secret of the beautiful tones. On leaving the building I found myself in a labyrinth of back streets and alleys and I realised I had tried to take a short cut to the source, which had not worked. I struggled through the dark, twisting maze of dirty streets and passages. Ominous shadowy figures lurked and the eerie sounds of the night echoed. For guidance and protection, I relied on my intuition and the faith that I knew what I was doing. Finally, I reached the original door through which I had first entered the cathedral. On re-entering I realised that the source of the sublime sound lay not in the heights of the spire, but in the depths, in the crypt below ground. Here was an encounter with the secret held by the Dark Twin. It showed that to reach the heights one has to negotiate the depths. I realised the importance of looking beyond the obvious. It is only by stepping off the main avenues of thought into the strange twisted ways beyond that we truly open up to a sense of the mystery, where the essence of creativity lies.

To be able to create anything new, one has to free oneself from habitual or rigid patterns of thought. The creative mind needs to be like mercury, fluid and able to morph from one thought shape to another, so that new angles and ideas can be formed. An art college teacher once told her students to always look at the shape of the spaces between the objects, rather than at the objects themselves. We have preconceived ideas of what things look like, so we need to get a fresh perspective to be able to see anything as if it were for the first time. We then have an honest view of it and we see it in its true form, and also in an exciting and inspiring new light, for anything freshly experienced transmits the vital energy of its magical essence.

Seeing anything for its true magic is the flowering of creativity in the mind. As William Blake wrote, "The tree which moves some to tears of joy is in the eyes of others only a green thing that stands in the way." So much in life is a matter of perception. C.S. Lewis describes a situation in his Narnia book *The Last Battle* where a number of characters find themselves in a paradise, while a group of dwarves sitting on the grass imagine themselves to be in a dark stable. There is no way that the others can persuade the dwarves otherwise. This is the problem of the prison of the mind. It stifles the flow of creative life, with the chains of depression, despair and fear, which at different times threaten to trap every one of us. The routine of everyday life itself can also dull our senses to the illuminated reality of the creative spirit if we are not careful. We dig a groove that reassures us, but also threatens to cut us off from the paths of exploration.

Anthony Grey, who was held hostage for two years in Peking during the Cultural Revolution, suffered psychological torment and depression, but he was able to be creative and he wrote insightful stories. In his book *What is the Universe In?* (first published as *A Man Alone*) he states that in many ways he was pushed out on to a metaphysical limb… "One's contact with mundane reality was more tenuous. The limb might well have cracked and sent one tumbling down into a new, undreamed of and infinite dimension of existence".

Once we are off the "beaten track", it becomes far more possible to push boundaries and cross over frontiers. The previously unimagined and impossible becomes attainable. When Orson Wells directed *Citizen Caine*, it was a new and exciting experience for him and he found original ways of doing things with film that had been thought to be impossible. His approach was fresh and unconventional. He was not hampered by the limitations of learned rules.

The creative mind also needs to explore an aspect of the bizarre in the strange corners of the back streets and the wild woods to feel the true freedom of inspiration. A French volcanologist fantasised that he was to build a boat that could take him speeding down the rapids of a lava flow! As Clarissa Pinkola Estés says in *Women who run with the Wolves*, "To create one must be willing to be stone stupid, to sit upon a throne of a jackass and spill rubies from one's mouth." The craziness of the Fool breaks through the barriers of the impossible into new realms and dimensions. The spirit of the wild, crazed god Dionysos inspires the creative mind. C.S. Lewis writes in *Surprised by Joy*, "Now I tasted the classics as poetry"... "Here was something very different from the Northerness"... "A new quality entered my imagination: something Mediterranean and volcanic, the orgiastic drum-beat"... "It was perhaps unconsciously connected with my growing hatred of the public school orthodoxies and conventions, my desire to break and tear it all." Here is a Christian writer, whose imagination nevertheless recognises the need for the anarchic freedom of the Dionysian spirit. William Blake's work also applauds the wild aspect of humanity. He writes in *The Marriage of Heaven and Hell*, "The reason Milton wrote in fetters when he wrote of Angels and God, and at liberty when of Devils and Hell, is because he was a true Poet, and of the Devil's party without knowing it." Along with the wild god Pan, Dionysos as god of the senses, ecstacy and revolt, becomes "the Devil" in Christian theology. However, Dionysos still pushes his way through to the imagination of any truly creative person, whatever their religion, for he frees the spirit from the chains of convention, with the threat of stagnation that accompanies it. He is the necessary chaos aspect of the Trickster. Out of the destructive flames of chaos rises the phoenix of creation, resplendent with the wonder, colour and vibrancy of a new birth.

Another way to leave the well-worn highway is to literally take off! That is, to mentally and spiritually rise above it. Tribal communities have traditionally believed that their shamans could fly. From that viewpoint, they could see everything from a much wider perspective. If the creative person can mentally fly then, like the shaman, he or she can take in the broader picture. From this aerial viewpoint, one can see for instance that the traveller fighting his way through a forest of strife will subsequently reach a green pasture of joy and peace. It is important for the creative person to transmit this wonderful message of hope to the desperate traveller, so that he does not give up. The medium of symbolic language, art or music communicates directly with the traveller's subconscious. His intuition then gives him a feeling of well being and encouragement.

. The ability to have an aerial vision enables one to sense the future at the same time as the past and present, to transcend the boundaries of time as well as space. While the ecstatic and painful experience of Dionysian inspiration gives the creative person a sense of direct involvement with intense emotions and sensations, the overview gained from the experience of mentally flying or floating gives a feeling of non-attachment. The level people are on most of the time exists on a different wavelength, which lies in the relatively comfortable area between these two points. The "off-beat" wavelengths are the best way for new, original avenues of thought, beauty and inspiration to flower and burst into being, but it means that the creative person, like the shaman or mystic, can often feel alienated and out of step with everyday life. For this reason he or she can be misunderstood or hurt, and can at times feel "odd", lonely or left out, beyond the companionship of the few who are on a similar wavelength. Also, because of the need for creativity to be open to all sensations, from the ecstatic inspiration of beauty, joy and truth to the harsh experiences of suffering and sadness, the creative person absorbs a lot of pain. Like many shamans, the creative person is a wounded soul.

Our ecstatic experiences can lead us directly to creative inspiration, but so can our moments of heartfelt sadness and despair. In reaching out for answers and help, we can find ourselves turning inwards and descending the caverns of our souls to the darkest recesses. Then we reach the place where our innermost feelings and our deepest knowledge reside within the source of our being. Here is where we find the creative melting pot, where the process the alchemists called "solve et coagula", as dissolve and fuse, disintegrate and reintegrate, or death and rebirth, occurs. It is where our experiences and emotions are transformed into a myriad of creative forms.

Here at the heart of the essential mystery of creativity and healing is the quality of Love, which emanates from the inner place where everything is understood, and where all is whole and at peace. William Wordsworth wrote, "Poetry is the spontaneous overflow of powerful feelings – it takes its origin from emotion recollected in tranquillity." The ancient Greek figure of Orpheus expresses perfectly the healing power of creativity, with its connection to inner tranquillity and love. Oliver Taplin in his book *Greek Fire* wrote, "Orpheus' enchanting music can bridge the gap between the human and the animal, even the inanimate world. It can bridge the gap between life and death: love combined with music defies mortality." The creative process unlocks and channels the light from within into beautiful forms, which soothe and heal the soul.

The Dark Twin leads us through our suffering to a place where the positive energy within is the transformative power. It is this energy that connects with the ecstatic experience, but it also transmutes the darkness of pain into a gift of heartfelt empathy for the woundings of everyone. The slow movement of J.S. Bach's Concerto for Two Violins in D Minor expresses the warmth of a spirit who knows deep sadness. But at the same time the music is so exquisite that it is soothing and uplifting. It is a reminder that the qualities of tranquillity, beauty and love are somewhere, if not in the present, then just around the corner, and always in one's heart.

The creative process involves the Dark Twin further when it uses the Dionysian energy of catharsis to express powerful, intense feelings. In this way, creativity directly expresses pain, enabling all who share in the experience to see their own hurt or anger reflected in it, and so sufferers are able to release their pent-up emotions through it. Here, we whirl with the Dervishes, we encounter Dionysos' frenzied Maenads, we dance with wild abandon to heavy rock music and we revel to the rousing sounds of Beethoven's Fifth Symphony. We feel the power of King Lear's crazed cries on the windswept heath, and we relive our darkest moments of anguish through the primal scream of ecstacy and delight. We feel the sense of our own pain as a shared experience, part of the rich, vibrant tapestry of life.

The whole creative process is therefore connected to the magical properties of the Healer, derived from the compassion that lies at the Source. It also keys into the deep knowledge of the Mystic, the sense of oneness with Life. That is why shamans of tribal communities have generally possessed all three qualities of the Healer, the Mystic and the Artist. Deeply linked to nature, Orpheus was a healer and mystic, as well as a musician. In the deepest sense, these three elements are inseparable.

Orpheus is traditionally connected to both the god Apollo and his dark counterpart Dionysos. He seeks the perfection of light, but is drawn into darkness, and eventually his head ends up in Dionysos' cave, while is lyre is laid in Apollo's temple. In a television interview, the controversial writer Salmon Rushdie said that the creative person resolves the paradox of life through synthesising seemingly irreconcilable opposites. Creativity unlocks the secret of the Sphinx, because the power of it enables us to touch the deepest mystery of the Dark Twin and to activate his powers of transformation.

The creative person transforms to Light whole areas of the unexplored continent of life's potential, opening up vistas of ideas, beauty and vitality, and connecting them back to the original Source in many new forms. By tapping into this divine Source, and by nourishing it, he or she becomes an increasingly powerful co-creator with the Spirit of Creation.

The Inspiration of Childhood

# THE INSPIRATION OF CHILDHOOD

Now he spoke of the 'aberration of our civilisation,' its loss of ecstacy, of the sense of the world as magical. 'Every child is aware of that until persuaded otherwise.'

*R. D. Laing: A Divided Self* by John Clay.

In childhood one often lives a kind of virtual reality. A child lives the wonder of any experience, whether it is an outing, a holiday, Christmas, a birthday, a pantomime, a film or a book. I remember how as a child I lived the books I read. I relished the taste of the hot melted cheese on fresh bread in Heidi's grandfather's little mountain home. I enjoyed the dangerous challenge of survival on Robinson Crusoe's tropical island. My fascination and absorption with C. S. Lewis' Narnia chronicles was so strong that it felt as if I had been through all the episodes myself. I could feel the frozen realm of the White Witch and the joyful release with the golden lion Aslan and his fantastic entourage of mythical creatures. I was struck by the wonder of witnessing the dawn of time and I wept at the death of an incredible world. I remember the magical realm of Narnia as vividly as the home of my childhood. Those books inspired me to paint pictures that surpassed my normal standard. They induced a deep sense of what I refer to as "cosy magic".

A wealth of creativity was unleashed because this virtual reality was moreover a heightened reality. With the child's ability to live in the present moment, uncluttered by heavy baggage from the past or concerns about the future, the experience of the world of imagination was direct and powerful.

The stories that inspired me did not only come from books, but also from my grandfather. The old and wise and the young and innocent often relate closely. In a dedication to the young Lucy Barfield at the beginning of *The Lion, the Witch and the Wardrobe*, C. S. Lewis writes, "you are already too old for fairy tales"... "But some day you will be old enough to start reading fairy tales again." My grandfather had reached the stage where he could once again connect closely with the mythopoeic world of the imagination, but with a lifetime's experience and the developed ability of the spirit of the bard.

Grandfather, or "Pok" as I knew him, had a deep knowledge of many old fairytales. He enhanced my dream world with colourful images of enchanted forests, evil sorcerers and shining palaces. He brought these tales to life so vividly that he could have received them directly from the very mouths of the dwellers of the Black Forest or the Hertz Mountains. Could it have been the souls of his own ancestors from the kingdom of Saxony coming through to him? An atmosphere of the spirits from the past clung to Pok's world, which itself extended back into another era. He had seen Queen Victoria as she passed by in her carriage and he had met Buffalo Bill. He was already an adult when the Titanic went down, and he lived through the traumatic experience of the trenches in the First World War. Perhaps his connection with a world gone by helped him to reach back to an even older time. His white busts of famous composers literally watched me walk by, as did the horned trickster-like faces on an old stone Etruscan urn he kept in the hallway.

The heart of Pok's realm was the attic, which could only be reached via a wooden ladder. In order to enter the main space, one had to first pass through a small anti-chamber. As the pungent musty smell pervaded my senses, I was filled with fascination as I caught glimpses of ageing yellow manuscripts and books. Here, amidst the shadows,

I could hear the whispering voices of old ghosts and living memories. It felt as if Pok's life had been a journey through space and time, like a travelling storyteller, gathering a host of spirits and legends on the way and finally arriving back at the original source, to inspire the very young.

There were many places and experiences that for me as a child took on a heightened reality and were raised in my imagination to mythic proportions. Gardens were transformed into whole lands of fantasy, full of dark caverns, imposing fortresses and shimmering lakes. Country lanes led deep into unexplored territory, where giants could lurk behind trees that loomed on either side, and the woodlands were populated with mythical beasts, dragons, leprechauns and fairies.

A child has a natural sense of the magical spirit of nature. The first tree at the entrance to Pok's wood, with its gnarled knotted trunk, was surely the ancient guardian of the wood and the huge beech tree in the centre was the King. I could feel the miraculous energy of eternal renewal in the mystical grotto at the source of the Seine. The first time I set eyes on the Alps at the age of four, I was struck by the strength of their awesome presence, as if the mountains themselves were beings to revere and to commune with. I had the strong urge to find my way both to the top and to the magical centre of these magnificent beings, so I could be fully at one with them. No wonder there are stories of the paradisiac valley in the heart of the Himalayas, and no wonder so many mountains have been hailed as sacred homes of the gods.

This sense of oneness with the spirit in nature is the mystical connection with the soul of life that we naturally feel as small children. We can lose it as we grow older, because we did not have the experience or intellectual capacity to understand the spirit we felt when so young and new to the world. So, as we grow we put away "childish fantasies" and become "realists". Also, repetition dulls the senses. It is whenever we experience something for the first time that we receive the full impact of its essential nature. It is vital to keep alive this sense of wonder and connection.

The Dark Twin within carries the fresh vision of the child like a seed germinating through to the adult self, at which point he encourages it to burst forth in a new dance of becoming. This dance includes original steps that can challenge the old order. When we feel the quickening of creative inspiration, we are once again entering the direct experience of life's spiritual source. Through poetry, music, art, dance, or any other form of creativity, we reconnect with the magical realm of our childhood, but now with the wisdom and ability to become co-creators with the power of creation. To quote the late nineteenth century American poet Charles Baudelaire, "Genius is nothing more than childhood recaptured at will... a childhood now equipped for self expression with manhood's capacities." Whenever any of us are tapping into that creative source, we are all sprinkled with the magical dust of what we call "genius", and the child within is our guide and inspiration.

# PART TWO

## VENTURING INTO THE DARK TWIN'S REALM

Preparing for the Journey

# PREPARING FOR THE JOURNEY

*All experience is an arch to build upon.*
Henry Brooks Adams

As a child, one has an automatic connection with the inner realm. As both T. S. Eliot and C. G. Jung have observed, we come to know that place of our beginnings after the passing of the years and the experience of exploration.

The spontaneity of the child and the excitement he or she feels through directly experiencing the sense of magic are a vital gift for us to hold on to. However, the child is in a state of ignorance regarding the complexity of life, and lives in the safety of the parents' protection.

We have to leave the wild and magical kingdom of childhood for the defended adult realm of earthly reality, in order to learn to be self-sufficient and responsible for our lives, to contribute to mankind's development and to live a full and productive life. In this realm we discover new horizons, we take gambles, we observe and we explore. Our journey in life takes us through each portal of the conscious realm, from the mechanics of the engine room to the secrets of the garden, and from the whirling fairground of society to the echoing halls of our personal joys and agonies. It is vital to experience the varied and sometimes cruel game of life, and to get to grips with the impact of the concrete physical world. It is important to travel, study, work, and play, to observe others on a train or in a street, to see the effect on people of money and power, and to dare to enter the dangerous dark alleys of poverty. We need to feel our highest and deepest feelings and to embrace every personal relationship with an open heart.

Through experiencing the world, we come to understand the patterns of living things, the ways of mankind and in particular the feelings and lives of those we care about. We also gain a sense of who we are, what we need to learn and what gifts we have to offer. Then, if we also follow our hearts we open ourselves up to both the pain and the ecstacy, which move us towards the threshold of the subterranean realm of the Dark Twin. We already connect with this place in our dreams and intuitions, and the child within never left it. Our moments of intense joy give us illuminating and tantalising glimpses of the magical realm of our long lost childhood, while the stabbing pains of our woundings and personal sacrifices lead us to the shores of the mythical river, the boundary between the protected life and the Great Unknown. We are then ready to receive the call to cross the river and enter the parallel universe.

The Parallel Universe

# THE PARALLEL UNIVERSE

*You yourself are even another little world and have within you*
*the sun and the moon and also the stars.*
Origen

The inner world that runs alongside everyday reality has existed from the beginning of our lives, for everything that occurs in our conscious life is reflected in our subconscious experience, and visa-versa. At times of crisis, change, discovery and challenge we hear the call to enter the deeper part of the lower realm. If we respond to the call, then the experience of that inner place intensifies and grows. Everybody in some way receives a call at a number of different points in their lives, including an inevitable call such as the recognition of the transition from childhood to teens in puberty. The sense that it is time to have a child is a calling, as is the sensation of falling in love. Regularly, we are being summoned to partake of a new experience of spirit and life, where there is a constant interplay between the dark and light universes.

Our exploration down through the layers of the subconscious can take a long time, invariably years. So, unless we are to disappear into the desert or wilderness as mystics, hermits or trainee shamans, we still continue to live on the conscious level with worldly involvement, but also with the guidance of the inner realm. What happens here is a developing manifestation of a parallel universe.

External events in our conscious lives immediately trigger a subconscious reaction. If a close friend or relative dies, a part of us dies with that person and we go through the dark valley in our state of mourning. If we refuse to mourn, then we impair our state of personal growth and well being. It is always damaging to refuse the call, whether it is to love, to be creative, to face a challenge, or to mourn. Individuals in tribal societies who have refused the call to become shamans have generally suffered prolonged illness and psychological trauma. In *Further Along The Road less Travelled* M. Scott Peck describes our inner/outer adventure as being like a journey across a desert. He states that if we give up and stop following the challenging call of life's stony road, we are metaphorically digging a hole in the sand and sitting in it. This psychic wilderness of inner stagnation cuts us off from our development and potential, and we increasingly suffer from a spiritual paralysis. On the other hand, if we continue to travel and to follow our callings, we begin to feel an increasing sense of the life force, until finally we rediscover the lost paradise we left behind.

Our callings often come as a reaction to external events, but equally they can act as a sign from within that we are ready to change things in our lives. They can actually trigger a whole new set of events. Sometimes, we feel the pull of a calling, and then an external event miraculously occurs to encourage us to face the challenge of the call from within. When we realise an inner need for change, the answer can strangely present itself to us in our outer circumstances. There are times when we think to ourselves "It really is time I sort that problem out", or "I realise I'm in a rut and I must find a new way". Then within days, or even hours, we see the ideal job advertised, the perfect offer comes through the door, the person of our dreams enters the room, or the appropriate challenge catapults itself into our lives. This is synchronicity between the two universes. C. G. Jung believed synchronistic events to occur during the most important phases of personal growth. This is where the miraculous mystery of the Dark Twin plays an active role, linking the inner world to the outer, and also linking the worlds of different individuals on a subconscious level.

Sometimes it is entirely up to us to act on an inner calling without any obvious help or prompting from without. We often have to motivate ourselves to follow that call, which is not easy. In primitive societies, when a person received a call to be a shaman because of latent powers within, it was his or her lonely path to follow it. The life of that person would then change completely. At certain times in all of our lives our subconscious spirit raises its voice and summons us to listen. Then it is for us to choose if we wish to face the challenge and embrace the change.

Often there is a sense of pressure. It is a knowledge that we receive from the depths of the inner chambers. We are only open to the call for a brief moment in time, and we must take hold of the opportunity before we lose it. This tends to happen when our lives are so deeply entrenched that we are in danger of losing the energy to initiate change. Also, the tide of events is constantly changing, as Shakespeare so aptly puts it in his *Julius Caesar*, "There is a tide in the affairs of men, which taken at the flood, lead on to fortune". There are particular moments when the time is right.

I once dreamed of receiving a message to descend a staircase through various levels. I wanted to put shoes on my feet, but somehow I knew that if I hesitated even for a moment, I would lose the opportunity. So, I descended barefoot. Finally I reached a door to a cellar. Once through there, descending the final staircase, I felt an intense sense of elation, for my paradigm had shifted. It is in this way that we can enter the deeper layers of the subconscious and embark on a dangerous but magical subterranean journey, which is generally reflected by a more precarious, yet more deeply rewarding way of life. Here it becomes clear how the dark and light universes mirror each other.

In my situation, I was being called to leave the cocoon of a safe, protected way of life, and to welcome the challenge of the Great Unknown. Only by entering this realm could I increase my creativity, experience and wider perspective on life. My subconscious universe now played a stronger part in my life than before. I was now exploring the depths of the subterranean forest, where many dangers lay in wait.

> Make your choice, adventurous stranger
> Strike the bell and bide the danger
> Or wonder, till it drives you mad
> What would have happened if you had.
> C.S. Lewis, *The Magician's Nephew*

I soon found myself embarking on risky projects. I was breaking into a dangerous forest in both worlds, full of pitfalls and wild beasts. There were times when I felt I could not take any more; too many rejections, too many upsets, too many mistakes and too many wolves. But often a rush of defiant energy would rise up from the fiery depths and explode, like the Tower in a deck of tarot cards. A fairy glen would then appear, glowing with the phosphorescent waters of Life. Here, I would gain fresh inspiration and hope, through a glimpse of the deep magic within the heart of the forest. From the shimmering waters would come the voice of my intuition telling me to keep going. Simultaneously, a new door would open in the conscious world in the form of a new friend, a helping hand, or a new opportunity.

Many tread a similar path. Some are brave enough to go further and enter the deepest layers of the subconscious realm. Discovering the unexplored roots within enables one to break through existing boundaries to reveal new discoveries, which burst forth like joyful fountains of truth and light into the world above. Great psychiatrists such as

C. G. Jung, and later R. D. Laing and Fritz Perls all took a step away from the beaten track, intensely explored their own inner worlds as pioneers of the mind, and broke through barriers to reveal new insights and approaches to psychological states. In *Memories, Dreams and Reflections*, Jung describes walls that divide as transparent. He knew how to use his own inner discoveries to bring to light a whole new level of psychological and spiritual understanding.

Creatively, the same procedure can take place. The musician who as a Black Sheep left the band explores a whole range of genres, and has a powerful relationship with his inner universe. Music often comes to him in dreams, and he remembers it in his waking state. Moreover, by literally flying in dreams and walking through walls, thereby finding a freedom from the restrictions of rigid thinking, he enables himself to break through musical boundaries. His visionary fusion of sounds, including a blend of contemporary and traditional music, gives birth to new forms and ideas in his work. His deeply enriched inner world also heightens his whole musical sense of the dramatic and of emotion, colour and atmosphere.

There is a constant interplay between the dark and light realms, strongly and clearly seen through creative expression, but experienced at some level in every aspect of life. The parallels operate like Alice's looking glass, or the characters and situations Dorothy meets in *The Wizard of Oz*, which are direct mythical reflections of the conscious world, where each character has his or her worldly counterpart. As Tom Chetwynd says in his *Dictionary of Symbols*, "Tartarus, by one account, is as far below HADES, the underworld of Greek myth, as Heaven was above earth"... "This shows a balance in which the worlds of the conscious mind are reflected in the depths below". By coming to a clear realisation of this phenomenon, we pay more attention to our inner voice, we listen out for the call, we look for the clues and we tune in to the reflecting patterns of the interplay between the two worlds. We can then feel a stronger sense of our potential, realising that the deeper we explore the subterranean realm, the more enriched our conscious lives become. As the barriers break down between the two universes, so do the blocks within our lives. We fly through walls, we break into unexplored territory, and we give birth to new forms and ideas.

The Threshold

# THE THRESHOLD

> The terrifying lions that guard the entrance to the inner chamber of the Palaeolithic cave, and later stand at the gates of temples, are expressly there as a warning: do not cross the threshold with a literal mind.
>
> Anne Baring and Jules Cashford

The great journey into the Inner Realm can be taken more than once in our lives, but each time we go through the process as if it was the first time. Once we have responded to the call to enter our parallel universe on the deeper level, the Ferryman takes us across the river to the Threshold, the yawning entrance to the Underworld.

Having braved failures and gained achievements in the worldly sphere, to cross the threshold it is necessary to take off the mantle of the outer persona that the world has built up, while still retaining the knowledge our experiences have given us. We therefore prepare to go through that portal with an openness of spirit, but also with the inner strength of the self-assurance we have developed and the wisdom we need to be able to confront and comprehend the challenge of the Realm of the Dark Twin.

The discarding of the unnecessary part of outer identity came up in repeated dreams I had where I lost the bag that carried my purse and personal belongings. Each time I retraced my steps in order to find it, but then I was never able to reach my destination and everything went wrong. Finally, in one dream I remembered that it was not a good idea to try to retrieve my bag, and I realised that I should go ahead without it. I had terrible difficulties forcing myself to leave it behind and to cross the threshold through a door into the room beyond. It was as if I had split into two, each side of myself battling with the other. However, once I had overcome my fearful clinging side, I succeeded in passing through the door and I felt a tremendous sense of achievement, freedom and elation. That was the last "bag" dream I had, for it was a lesson learned and a portal entered.

I also had an interesting threshold dream that dealt with the strength and wisdom we require, along with a strong sense of our intuition. In order to enter a large temple-like building, I had to walk towards a fierce tribal warrior, adorned with painted face and plumed feathers and wielding a long sharp knife. I convinced myself I had to trust he was not real, that he was just a testing force. So, holding on to the courage of my intuition, I managed to walk through him as if he was nothing but a ghost or a hologram.

Monsters such as the three headed dog Cerberus, are invariably mythic figures that guard the entrance to the Underworld and challenge anyone who wishes to enter. They are monsters of our egos, but like the incorporeal warrior, they are demons of our fears. We are particularly afraid of the unknown. This terror has to be overcome if we are to take as much as one step into the unexplored lands and unchartered waters of our inner selves.

Our victory over the guardian monster gives us increased confidence in our intuition and frees us from the heaviest shackles of our worldly ego. However, we are still armed with the ingenuity gained from our experience in the conscious realm. The resourceful Odysseus entered Hades with the wisdom of experience, and Theseus accepted Ariadne's thread with the realisation that we have to keep a constant link with the conscious realm in order to avoid losing ourselves in the dark maze below. If we remain balanced and centred, we are ready to face the awesome challenge of the Underworld, with all the paradoxical riddles and tests that lead us toward the ultimate experience of death and transformation.

Helpful Spirits

# HELPFUL SPIRITS

We catch the fractal waves of similar folk in the field of our own particular style and history. We may be similarly quickened by the dominant Essence that comprehends the family of which we are a part.
Jean Houston

Once our hearts are opened by our woundings and the crossing of a threshold has freed our minds from the shackles of worldly and material expectations, we are able to embrace the love and assistance of kindred spirits and guides, who will help us throughout our journey.

As we descend into the depths of our inner realm, we become aware of these souls. It is the spiritual family to which we belong. It is like tuning into a radio wavelength. When we connect with someone on a similar vibration to ourselves, even if that person is a long way off physically, they can reach out to touch us on the unseen plane of existence.

A deep connection can exist between people who are strangers on the conscious plane, which could be an explanation for why occasionally we meet someone, and along with a strong feeling of empathy, we sense that somehow we already know them. We subsequently discover to what degree we are on a "wavelength" with that person. It is as if we are drawn together by some magnetic force. One woman, who is highly tuned to the feelings of others, has dreamed of people she had not yet met at the time. These were those she was destined to become close to, such as the man she later married.

Invariably, people have telepathic experiences with those they are closest to, especially when they need help. There are many examples of this happening between siblings and in particular with twins. In one case, a man was electrocuted, and his twin miles away felt the shocks at that very moment as if it was happening to himself. Siblings have been known to assist one another in dreams. In one case, two sisters shared a complex dream, right down to the finest detail of the events. Parents often have telepathic experiences with their children, and a mother in particular often knows from a distance if a child of hers is in distress. In many such cases, our guiding spirits are those of the living, but it is possible they are sometimes the dead.

The Australian Aborigines have the belief that spirits of the dead assist them. This concept is also part of ancestor worship beliefs around the world from various tribal cultures to the Japanese Shinto religion. Many individuals can feel a connection with spirits from the past too. A musician, for instance, may feel inspired with the spirit of either Bach or Hendrix running through his veins! He could well have subconsciously tapped into the wavelength of those spirits. Whether these spirits actually exist, or whether they are figments of our active imagination does not necessarily matter, for if the aid or the inspiration is effective, then we are at least being helped by a sense of these souls from the inner realm. When the medium Eileen Garrett asked spirits if it was them she was seeing, or if what she was seeing was from her brain, they replied that it was both.

My father, who died over twenty years ago, has appeared to my sister and I occasionally in our dreams to encourage us in times of doubt. These could have been nothing more than ordinary dreams, but at least a couple of them shifted our paradigms to such a degree that clearly something of psychic significance had occurred. In one dream of mine he handed me a multi-stringed cylindrical musical instrument. "You can play the guitar," he said, "But this gift here will help you learn all these extra strings". He then explained that he had to return to the place he had come from. When I awoke, I knew I needed to expand my creative horizons, and it gave me a whole new lease of life. Even if it was only metaphorical, it was still the spirit of my father, and the impact was effective and powerful.

In the spiritual realm, it appears that the "fractal wavelength" not only crosses cultural boundaries, but also breaks down the barriers between the living and the dead. It is the point where all spirits meet, and where we look to our greater spiritual family, a circle of souls, for support and guidance. All these connect with our own inner spirit, the powerful magical source that dwells within each and every one of us.

*The Inner Spirit*

# THE INNER SPIRIT

Each of us has this inner space, but during the lives of most people, it becomes smaller and smaller. As we go through life, the world around us tries to fill up and kill this inner space, your Spirit Lake.

Olga Kharitidi

I had been walking for a time, before I came across some beautiful old trees with enormous gnarled trunks and large shining leaves. Passing through these, I entered an ancient forest. It had a quality of deep magic. A voice told me that the forest had shrunk in size, with fields taking up one side and a motorway cutting off the other. However, the forest itself was still as alive with mystery and enchantment as it had ever been. I was told that I could rescue the endangered forest if I was able to find the magical stag that inhabited it. There were a number of deer there, but I intuitively knew which was my special stag as soon as I set eyes on him. We approached each other. The noble face of the stag looked directly at me, and then to my surprise became the face of a woman with intense, shining eyes. This being then spoke to me. The message was for me to keep in contact with my inner self, to nurture it, and to help it to thrive and grow back to its original size. The dream was powerful and thought provoking.

The Spirit Lake and the Enchanted Forest both symbolise the place inside every one of us where we find the seat of our soul, our life force and our creativity. It is the essence of our being, and like the source of a river in a cavern, it needs to be constantly replenished. This place is represented in the tarot pack as the star card, where the waters of life are revitalised in the Subterranean Realm, to give hope and inner strength to a depleted soul. A musician once dreamed of a man who irrigated a dried up lake, until it was again full of water teaming with life. This gave rise to a whole new flood of creativity.

There are various ways in which this inner place of vital soul energy can be eroded. Others can drain our life-blood when we allow them to prey on us as psychological vampires. Invariably this happens because of our lack of self- confidence, involving fear or guilt or desperation to please. A deadening tiredness begins to set in because all the joy of life and creativity we possess is being sucked dry.

It is often society itself that threatens to take us over. It leads us to feel that the outer world is of paramount importance, and sometimes ·even that there is no other place to consider. In C. S. Lewis' *The Great Divorce*, a large man representing a false front or "actor", holds a little man symbolising the person's true nature on a chain, like a dog on a lead. They vie with each other. Eventually, the large man grows to such powerful proportions as the other shrinks, that he is able to pick the little man up, put him into his mouth and swallow him whole.

Society itself swallows a lot of people up, and in this way it is like a giant or a false god. The god of money and possessions can rule people. There are those that live in constant terror of losing their wealth. One couple never left their house for as much as one night if it was unattended, even though they had burglar alarms and neighbours close by. These people are in a prison of the mind. A businessman can become completely absorbed with his career, placing it above all else. The struggling unemployed person can be swallowed up with anxiety about debts, and may then spend hours watching soaps on television to escape the drudgery of life. The world around us makes it very difficult to keep in touch with the lifeblood of our inner spirit world.

Having introduced the reader to the Spirit Lake, Kharitidi writes, "Later you will also learn that there is an important Inner Being who lives there. You will need to meet and understand this Spirit Being." The man who irrigated the lake was that for the musician. The talking stag-woman was that for me. This was an all embracing creature both male (shown by the stag's antlers) and female (the face and voice), animal and human. This spirit was putting me back in touch with my true self. It was the conduit through which my inner-self could speak and it was the personification of a deep-seated wisdom we all possess in a place where spirit, soul and nature meet and all is one. Kharitidi refers to this spirit as "your Heart Self". In the heart of my forest was the magical stag. Perhaps it is no coincidence that a special kind of stag is referred to as "the White Heart".

The inner guide appears in our dreams, thoughts and our subterranean journey to help us nurture and replenish our spiritual source, so that the river of our life can once again flow with the full force of creative vitality and joy. The reservoir can again become plentiful. The forest of our personal inner growth again thrives, in its turn revealing its host of mystical deities and creatures, which also serve to inspire and lead us toward a greater awareness. Some of these are creatures that present us with a difficult or dangerous test, in order to prepare us for the awesome final goal of our quest.

Ride the Wild Tiger

# RIDE THE WILD TIGER

Life is like a wild tiger.
You can either lie down and
Let it lay its paw on your head,
Or sit on its back and ride it.
(Unknown)

I often dreamed of a tiger. In my first dream, I was in a wild wooded place. The tiger came up to me and spoke with a voice of deep wisdom. He told me to learn how to handle him in his raw, wild state. From that moment onwards, in subsequent dreams, he was a threatening wild animal I had to learn how to face and control. I failed repeatedly through my attempts to ignore, or to escape, or to push the tiger away. He would always attack.

The wild tiger is a dangerous force. His breath scorches our skin and his teeth shine with hungry anticipation. He is the devouring monster within, and he will stalk us at every turn. However, if we bring him under our control, he gives us the necessary strength we need to face the most difficult challenges of our lives. Without his energy, we are most often overcome by our fears, but when we harness his force to our thoughts and when we integrate him into our hearts, he feeds our confidence and our personal source of power.

The paradoxical problem of facing the tiger is that we need to have enough courage in the first place to deal with him! Initially, it is necessary to perceive him as a mirror that reflects the strength we already possess, and we have to have the faith that we are in with a fighting chance. Once we overcome our fear enough to face him, we can disarm his destructive energy and transform it into a positive drive that we can absorb. In this sense, we befriend him. As with a rider breaking in a wild horse, we take control of him, while simultaneously tuning into his nature and his rhythms. We are initiated into his mystery. He leads us back to our own naked wildness and we recognise his drive and power as our own. With his spirit running through our veins, we conquer irrational fears and anxieties, and the control we need to harness his energy gives us the shamanic power of divine mastery, through which transformation becomes possible.

Brian Keenan experienced wrestling with the wild monster force within as a form of aggressive madness, while being held in captivity as a hostage in Beirut. As a "musical delirium" was taking him over, he remembered that "you do not overcome by fighting, you only concede the victory to the madness within. You overcome by going beyond it". In effect, he joined its spirit energy by dancing to its rhythm, yet in doing so he was able to gain control over it. "I danced and danced until the music had to keep up with me"... "I was the master of this music"... "I felt myself alive and unfearful. I was the pied piper who was calling the tune". And so he defeated the monster of subterranean frenzy, while simultaneously transforming its powerful energy to form an effective magic. This increased the strength and vitality he desperately needed to cope with what became four years of imprisoned hell, and it also deepened his connection with the spirit of life.

As Keenan's experience shows, the tiger force does not necessarily reveal itself in animal form. Essentially, it is raw Dionysian energy, which is animal in its nature but can be experienced as pure sensation. It is a powerful gift from the Dark Twin, incorporating the paradoxical nature of his personality. To absorb the tiger's energy and properties, we have to be strong enough to trust in our intuition, so we can reach out to take hold of his strength and make it our own. While we conquer him, we also befriend him and honour him as a powerful god in the depths of our psyche. He is the most dangerous challenge we face on our descent and journey, until we reach the central core of the subterranean realm, where the pure essence of the Dark Twin lies in wait.

Letting Go

# LETTING GO

He who binds himself to a joy
Doth the winged life destroy
But he who kisses the joy as it flies
Lives in Eternity's sunrise.
William Blake

The challenge of confronting the aggressor is not the only fear we face on our inner journey. Courage is also needed for endurance, taking risks, and letting go. With each test we pass, we walk through another gateway. Letting go is difficult. Throughout our lives we develop many attachments. Some of these are healthy and constructive, while others are not. It is a problem if we neglect other important and nourishing aspects of our lives. If an attachment to our work becomes all embracing, then relationships can suffer, or an all too demanding relationship can stifle creativity.

Another difficult situation occurs when the time has come to let go. Children have to let go of their dependence on their parents as they grow up, and equally parents need to allow their children to spread their wings, for otherwise the children's growth is stunted. To quote Kahlil Gibran's *The Prophet*, "You are the bows from which your children as living arrows are sent forth".

Attachments can become sinister if their basis is that of control or fear, and these are often very difficult to shed, because at the root is often trauma, which happened in the past and in some cases has been repeated. Trauma often leads to a diminished level of confidence, and with that a need to cling to a prop that can be like the very thing that caused the trauma in the first place! One young woman, who has always gone for abusive relationships, has repeatedly attached herself to men who beat her. Originally her father beat her. When we are small children we see our parents as "God", because we are dependent on them for our survival. Therefore, if they abuse us, we feel that we are inferior because we cannot obtain their approval. Later, we choose a partner who turns out to be the next person to treat us badly. On one level we are subconsously still trying to "get it right", so that this substitute parent might finally bless us with his or her approval, and on another level we choose abuse because we feel unworthy. This kind of attachment is a negative syndrome that holds us back from flowering to our full potential.

School had traumatised one young girl, who for a long time was not able to shake off the demoralising influence of a school she had attended. Many years after leaving the place, she dreamed she was in the school grounds. The building was about to be demolished. She felt the heavy negative spirit of it threatening to draw her inside like a magnetic force. She purposefully turned and walked away. Something told her that however tempted she was, she must not look back at the building. With difficulty, she managed not to. As she turned a corner at the top of the street, the whole scene changed. She had entered an entirely new place.

The message of "Don't look back" is an ancient one. It comes up, for instance, in the myth of Orpheus, who loses his wife Eurydice to the land of the dead forever when his trust fails him and he turns to check if she is behind him. Lot's wife in the biblical story finds it difficult to lose her attachment to her old home and does not trust the message that it is being destroyed, so she turns to look back and is consequently petrified into a pillar of salt. These stories express the psychological difficulty we experience when our attachments stop us from simply trusting and letting go.

Clarissa Pinkola Estés writes in *Women who Run with the Wolves*, "it is this pain, this severing, this 'not having a foot to stand on,' so to speak, this no home to go back to, that is exactly what is needed to start over, to start fresh, to go back to the handmade life, the one carefully and mindfully crafted by us every day". We need to let go of that which holds us back from flowering to our full potential, whether it be an old worn out habit, something we have outgrown, or any experience or relationship that holds us in the iron grip of negative programming. Sometimes we are stuck in a situation where we have little or no choice, if for instance we are caught in a poverty trap or if we bare a responsibility to another person or people whose needs are greater than our own. However, even in the most repressive of situations, when we cannot physically walk away, we can still work on freeing our minds. As a hostage, Anthony Grey wrote that he dreamed himself out of his confining walls. Brian Keenan states that his own captors were more imprisoned than he was, because their attitudes and fears trapped them. They were literally prisoners of the mind.

As the Sumerian goddess Inanna goes through each gate of the Underworld, she sheds either jewellery or an article of clothing. Each time we shed a ball and chain we believe to be a prop we depend on, we too pass through a gate to a new level of experience. As Inanna discovers, it is a process that takes one ever closer to the naked nucleus of the inner-self.

Taking the Plunge

# TAKING THE PLUNGE

It is vain to say human beings ought to be satisfied with tranquillity; they must have action; and they will make it if they cannot find it.

Charlotte Brontë

My world was stifling me. I tried to get out of it but I was unable to move without bumping into a wall or reaching a precipice. I looked over the edge of a high cliff. I sensed that the world down there was a better place. I did not know if I would survive the fall, but I took a deep breath and jumped. A chilling fear gripped me as I plummeted downwards. Then suddenly I felt released and elated. I realised that I could control my fall, so I was able to land safely in water and then swim ashore. I found myself in a new and brighter universe. In this dream, I took the plunge.

The trust required for us to let go, we also need to take a risk. In fact, the two generally go hand in hand, like two sides of a coin. We let go of an old situation when we dive into a new one. In taking the plunge, we are also facing the fear of rejection and failure. We do not know for sure whether or not we will be able to cope with our new situation. It is our trust in our intuition that helps to guide us and give us strength.

The risks we take carry us through to another level, in both our subconscious and our worldly lives. Invariably, we find that we regret the things we did not do much more than the times we took risks, even if some of them did not work out, because they were still part of a learning process. When we pull back through giving in to our fears, we feel weakened. However, if we have the courage to take action, we generally gain strength and confidence, and our spirits feel more of a sense of freedom.

We are often terrified in life to cross that line. Whether we plan to ask someone out, or to apply for a new job, or to start a new life elsewhere or with a new partner, we all fear rejection, failure or disappointment. We are about to dive into the untested and unknown. The film *Out of Africa* shows how Karen Blixen had no idea what life would be like running a farm in Africa when she set forth. It could have turned out to be a disaster, but it became the experience of a lifetime. It is the point when our lives become an adventure, whether in a small or a big way, that we really embrace life.

It is equally important to take the plunge for the sake of our inner journey, for the subterranean world is like an onion. Every section is the unknown, a new experience we need to be prepared to face, but each time we successfully pass through from one to the next, we feel elated with the extra magical gift of the inner wisdom we receive. Opening ourselves up to the challenges of our repeated callings, we listen more and more to the voice of our hearts, the "Heart Self", and we are therefore increasingly able to express our love and to give it to others. We also need to take risks to develop our strength so that we can negotiate the inner path, which becomes increasingly difficult, as we move towards the centre.

The Way

# THE WAY

Knowledge itself is power.
Francis Bacon

The process of our journey through the subterranean realm is not only a matter of crossing the threshold, finding helpful entities and passing dangerous tests. It is a world of infinite complexity, and so we can easily lose our way in its dark entangled forests or its echoing labyrinthine passages. There are countless time zones, many universes to be explored, endless stories to be enacted and millions of players waiting in the wings to play their parts. There are also numerous ways in which we can find ourselves stuck down blind alleys of confused thoughts, or we can be tempted off the path of our journey by the fairground of excitement and short term amusement. Moreover, we are in danger of being overwhelmed by the impact of a deluge from our unconscious energy, which threatens to sweep over us like a tsunami.

For us to see clearly the route of our journey, and to be able to explore the wonders and challenges of the Dark Twin's world without being defeated by its complexity, we have to find the clue. It is necessary to give it a form and to discover the pattern it offers each of us as individuals. Mythology itself provides an overall pattern. It gives meaning to the chaos within.

Odysseus' arduous journey from Troy to his homeland is a typical example of how myth takes us through the experience of dealing with the vast sea of our unconscious. He overcomes trials, steers a narrow course

114

between the equally destructive forces of Scylla and Charybdis, resists the temptations of Circe and the sirens and faces the very depths of the Underworld itself. He displays the courage, ingenuity, balance and endurance necessary to negotiate the dangerous route through the inner realm.

Like myths, dreams also perform the task of guidance. Because they are personal, they give us particularly useful and clear instructions. Here, we need to understand the message and to use our intuition to decide whether the dream is a fear dream, a wish fulfilment dream, or a message of clear guidance. The pattern that emerges from our dreams becomes the path we follow.

The main clue exists in the form of the thread. When we have become confused by a book we are reading we say we have "lost the thread" of the story. The thread is our "yellow brick road" (Wizard of Oz), our path through the story. We lose the thread and we lose our way.

Brian Keenan found a way to cope with his dangerous exploration into the depths of the landscape of the mind by discovering what he himself described as "threads". He found himself "helplessly lost" in that strange universe. He writes, "But I could not stop, for to see what has previously been invisible is powerfully captivating". However, then he saw that "in all this confusion some veins of life held everything together" and he suddenly felt a sense of himself as "a whole human being". A deeper knowledge had revealed itself to him.

To be drawn into this inner world of miracles, yet to be clear headed enough to take hold of the thread and see the way is the state of one who has reached a point of some degree of balance within, and therefore a sense of wholeness. The thread creates wholeness in another sense too, because it integrates male with female aspects. Ariadne, with her feminine flexibility and intuition, gives the winding thread to Theseus, with his masculine direction and drive, for his venture into the dark labyrinth of the Minotaur. The thread also makes us whole by connecting our conscious to our subconscious. It is like an umbilical chord to the conscious realm, enabling the explorer not only to return to the upper world, but also to keep a clear sense of individual purpose in the lower world.

Scientists have discovered that during out-of-body experiences, people are in both a conscious and a subconscious state at the same time. This is where the umbilical chord to consciousness manifests itself physically. Consciousness interacting with the subconscious also happens in lucid dreaming. In all the dreams I had of retracing my steps to retrieve my bag, I was following repeated patterns of subconscious insecurities. I was lost in a repetitious dream loop. However, when in one dream I remembered how all had gone wrong whenever I had turned back for my bag in previous dreams, the message was from my conscious mind, as it joined forces with the voice of my intuition from the subconscious. The problem was resolved and I crossed a threshold into a new area of inner experience.

The need to keep a thread or link connecting us to both our conscious selves and our intuition is expressed in a story in C. G. Jung's *Man and his Symbols*. Prince Hatim Tai is almost drowned by water in a bath, but when he grabs the centre-stone of the cupola, the water disappears and he finds himself in a desert. He has effectively saved himself from being overwhelmed by his subconscious world by grabbing hold of his conscious mind. However, he subsequently has to let go and trust his intuition and instinct when he shoots an arrow with his eyes shut, in order to bring life back to his world.

The solid square stone symbolism of consciousness in the centre of the unconscious realm was clearly depicted in a dream I had when I was trying to find a new level of awareness in order to deal with my life. I found myself in a world controlled by evil. The only way to get out was to journey to the centre of it. Here I found a dark forest. In the middle of the forest was an ancient ruined city. In the midst of the ruins I found an ancient Greek theatre, with its round orchestra, the dance floor. A cube shaped stone altar stood in the centre. A voice told me that this was the key to my quest.

Like the Prince Hatim Tai story, the above dream not only expresses the need to keep a grip on our solidity and conscious self, but it also shows the onion like nature of our inner journey. This is another clue to the pattern of our subconscious experience. We peal away layers as we enter each deeper level, and it is only by heading for the centre that we can work towards finding the final resolution through transformation.

In the Sumerian story of the fertility goddess Inanna's descent into the underworld, she reaches each layer via a gate. There are seven gates to the centre, and as she sacrifices a garment at each gate, she is preparing herself for the next level. We recognise these gates at points of challenge in our subconscious experience. In our dreams, each gate can be depicted as a gate, a door, a bridge, or any boundary between two different environments.

The labyrinthine journey towards the centre is often depicted as a spiral, the thread working its way around each ring and inwards. Connecting the concept of the onion with the spiral, we see a pattern. Each time the spiral returns to the point in line with the threshold, there is another gate to enter that presents a new challenge and a further test. It is a circular, yet progressive process.

The spiral factor is a paradox in itself. It encompasses the mirror we experience in the parallel universes of our lives. The higher we climb our road of trials, the further we descend to explore the dark labyrinth of our inner world. The wider and the broader our experience, our knowledge and our view on life, the closer we get to the inner core of our being. C.S. Lewis described the world of the afterlife in his book *The Last Battle* as being like an onion, "except that as you go in and in, each circle is larger than the last".

Therein lies the true mystery of the journey towards the centre. We follow the thread while we explore the labyrinth, our journey through the inner realm guides us through our waking experience, and the deeper we go, the more we embrace the breadth of existence.

Breaking into the
Inner Sanctum

# BREAKING INTO THE INNER SANCTUM

*The ultimate dragon is within you, it is your ego clamping you down.*
Joseph Campbell

The Inner Sanctum is where the Dark Twin lies in wait. It is the dragon's lair, guarded by his bloodthirsty minions. It is the place of death and rebirth. It is the belly of the whale, through whose teeth we have to pass with the same courage and ingenuity Jason needed to have when he negotiated the Argo through the clashing rocks.

The first threshold into the Inner Realm is not easy to pass through, as we are entering a different state of being, so a major shift of consciousness has to take place. Each subsequent gateway or door that we reach throughout our journey into this realm poses its own challenge, but it is the final one into the Inner Sanctum itself that is the most powerful, the most formidable and the most resistant.

Nature itself forms this deeply rooted pattern. For sperms that have succeeded in negotiating their way up through all the obstacles within the vagina, the most difficult task is that of finding their way in through the folds of the wall protecting the space containing the egg. The archetypal experience of the pattern of the inner journey has therefore existed within each and every one of us from the point of conception. It is a deep knowledge, which is indeed primal.

We all experience this phenomenon in our dreams. In one dream, I observed birds flying at a window of a house that had a negative atmosphere. They were intent on freeing the trapped spirit inside. The ones that hit the window with their soft bodies were instantly killed. However, those that hit the window directly with their piercing beaks cracked the glass. I realised that if this process carried on long enough, the persistent birds would finally succeed in breaking through the glass.

In *The Prophet,* Kahlil Gibran wrote, "Your pain is the breaking of the shell that encloses your understanding". We are often trapped by our fear to break through the walls of our personal prisons, because we can be so traumatised by the problems that have trapped us that we can develop an even greater terror of the unknown freedom. We are also afraid that if we fail in our attempts, then the situation might become even worse than if we had left it alone. The birds that were killed in the dream must have been these failed attempts, but the dream was showing the importance of persistence, for we often have more than one chance, and there are victories as well as failures. We can eventually succeed. The glass might shatter and wound us and the masonry might fall around our ears, but if we are resolute we can overcome the pain and deal with the truth that is released.

A young man, who had been trying to resolve a personal problem for some time, had a dream in which he had been climbing the slopes of a mountain, but had now reached a sheer rock face leading to the top. He saw a wooden door in the side of the rock and was told he had to enter it in order to reach the top. The inner voice informed him that he would need to negotiate volcanic activity inside, while making his way upward. However, he had to first work out the clue to opening up the wooden door, which was firmly locked. In our everyday lives, the symbolic locked door, gate or last threshold, is generally the final major block to the process of resolving a problem or issue. To enter the Inner Sanctum, we invariably have to take a risk of some magnitude, perform a test of shamanic proportions, use our most skilful ingenuity, or even open up Pandora's box of all the things we never dared to expose before. We face the demon here that stands in the way of our liberation, and we need to force our way through his gate of horror.

In the tarot deck, it is the Devil card that symbolises this last and most powerful block before the point of breakthrough and transformation. It is a deep resistance to change. In *Seventy-Eight Degrees of Wisdom,* Rachel Pollack states that it is precisely when we are moving towards our liberation that "we feel our unhappiness and the limitations of our lives most strongly. Before you can slip off the chains you must become conscious of them. Therefore, when people who are undergoing some process of liberation – say, when leaving home, psychotherapy or a difficult divorce – they often find themselves far more unhappy than when they blindly accepted their oppressed condition. Such a period can be crucial to a person's development. If one can survive it, one will emerge much happier and with a more developed personality. Sometimes we can find the period of transition unbearably painful and slip back to our chains". We need to hold on to our strong sense of the path of our hearts and our inner selves, the treasure the dragon is sitting on in the Inner Sanctum.

In many ways the final threshold acts as a resistant magnetic force, which gets stronger as we push our way through. J.R. Tolkien exemplified this phenomenon well in his *The Lord of the Rings.* The hobbits Sam and Frodo are trying to get into the centre of evil power, the land of Mordor, in order to destroy the ring. They first have to make a particularly hazardous trip through the entrance to this inner realm, where sits a forbidding mountain. As they negotiate this mountain and then approach the core of Mordor, they find their task increasingly difficult, because the negative power of the ring grows the closer it gets to the source. This power drains the energy and the resolve of Frodo, the bearer of the ring. He has to hold firm to his quest, to himself and to the positive support of his companion, Sam, in order to pass through the powerfully negative force.

The unlocking of this last gate is the final peeling away of our self-preserving ego, our protection against the full force of the negativity we wish to overcome. For the Sumarian goddess Inanna, it was the rejection of her final piece of clothing. To cross this threshold, we have to be spiritually naked, so that every part of ourselves sees and feels everything. As we enter the inner sanctum, we are initiated into the realm of the ultimate test, where the ghosts of all our fears fly in our faces and where the full impact of our task hits us directly. Here our deepest anxieties pull us like magnets towards the pit of despair where, as in a game of Snakes and Ladders, we might slide back down to the point our quest began, or worse still, into a self destructive downward spiral. Here, the Dark Twin waits to greet us, with hungry anticipation.

A Message of Transformation

# A MESSAGE OF TRANSFORMATION

As Dante puts it, the entrance to purgatory is at the deepest
point of hell.
Edward C. Whitmont

The strength and ingenuity required to push through
the final resistant threshold into the Inner Sanctum is
needed even more once inside. It is here that the Dark
Twin meets us as our own inner beast. Whether we have to
kill the dark aspect of ourselves with force through the
light of our heroic consciousness, or whether we sacrifice
our ego to the darkness, we need to take the risk of an
inner death to make it possible for rebirth and
transformation to take place.

Having gone through all the trials and tests, we
should now be ready to confront our Dark Twin. He waits
for us in the murky depths, but his teeth gleam, reflecting
the light we radiate from our positive energy. Without
that, his darkness would be all embracing. We would not
see him coming and he would suck us in like a black hole.
Even when he surrounds us with darkness, as within the
belly of the whale, we should still be able to protect
ourselves and negotiate our path with the light we carry.
He has many forms and he is androgynous, so he can
equally be male, like the Minotaur, or female, like the
Gorgon Medusa. At best he fills us with a sense of awe.
Most often, he is a terrifying apparition.

Sometimes, in this guise, the Dark Twin personifies
our worst fears, which we have to overcome in order to
gain confidence and release the flow of our inner growth
from the blockage of terror and doubt. Olga Kharitidi in

*Entering the Circle* explains her experience of confronting a circle of flames and men intent on murder. She describes her terror, but goes on to say, "Then, from out of nowhere, a simple understanding comes into my mind. This place and men surrounding me are all creatures of my own fears"... "I step confidently towards the drunken men. The red flames fade away, and the men first shrink into small amorphous shapes and then disappear entirely."

The monster we meet in the depths is often our own aggression, whether aimed outwardly towards others, or internally towards ourselves as negative complexes or chronic anxiety attacks. It is depicted as the Monster of the Id in the science fiction film *Forbidden Planet*. In this case, it is a manifestation of suppressed aggression, which its owner has to eradicate with the power of his mind. This bestial force is often killed with an equivalent aggression to its own in myths and legends, whether it is St. George slaying the dragon, or Theseus stabbing the Minotaur to death. Here, we have to ally ourselves with the strength of our "animus" hero as the positive male drive we all possess. But we still need to carry with us the protection of our feminine intuition. This is symbolised by Athena's reflecting shield, which gives us the opportunity to see the Gorgon without being turned to stone by the direct impact of her gaze, or Ariadne's thread, which enables us find our way back out of the labyrinth.

Sometimes the monster we destroy is simply the threat of stagnation. As Hermann Hesse wrote in *Demian* that for a birth to occur, a world has to be destroyed. Even the womb itself, the very life-creating force, becomes a life-threatening situation once it is time for birth.

In some dreams, myths and stories it is the main character's ego that is destroyed. This is symbolised as a personal sacrifice, which leads to a rebirth. If the hero within us kills the monster, he removes the block to our development. If we allow ourselves to be metaphorically consumed by the monster, we are taking an even bigger risk. We are entering an even deeper realm, which requires us to come to an understanding of the dark power within, so that we can be reborn with the essence of its mystery within us.

Stories like *Jonah and the Whale* and *Pinocchio* involve the transformation of the one on the quest, through his entering a monster's body. Both cases deal with personal sacrifice as the eradication of an inflated ego. The living doll Pinocchio has been through many trials already, and so is now ready to embrace the challenge the monster presents. Pinocchio realises the nature of his tomb when he uses his trickster ability to make a fire, so that the whale has to open his mouth, and escape is then possible. Moreover, he subsequently sacrifices his life to save his father from the whale's hungry jaws. He dies to his old life, to embrace a new one that is more fully enriched. This metaphorical death and self sacrifice comes up in many legends, whether it be the belly of the whale or the heart of the Underworld itself, the devouring jaws of Hades.

Sometimes, it is a character that is already evolved spiritually, who performs an act of self-sacrifice, invariably in order to save the lives of others. The enlightened wizard Gandalf in Tolkien's *The Lord of the Rings* throws himself into a pit with a monster in order to rescue his companions. He is later resurrected as an even more highly developed being. Once the goddess Inanna has been through the seven gates she meets her counterpart Ereshkigal, the goddess of death. Here, Inanna allows herself to be killed, with the deep knowledge that her life will be restored and renewed with the vital essence she requires for summer to return to the world above. She possesses an inner knowing, as well as the strength of both determination and faith.

As Richard Bach writes in *Illusions*, "What the caterpillar calls the end of the world, the master calls a butterfly". If we are to go through any major life change, we need to be prepared to allow our ego to be broken down, so that we no longer cling to our cocoons. Whether it be drug dependency, a bad home life, or a depressing place of work, these cocoons are the blocks of apparent security that prevent us from moving forward. We need to face the ultimate fear of the death force, as well as the skeletons we once shut in the deepest recesses of our hearts as the original painful experiences that knocked our self confidence, making us insecure and afraid of change. This would have also led to a child-like dependency on others for our sense of identity or feeling of self-importance, and for us to become victims of negative, abusive situations. What we require is the honesty of self-awareness, the strength of purpose, a sense of our own self-worth, and faith in the miracle of the power of transformation. This occurs when we allow the master within to divulge his or her wisdom. Within every Pinocchio is an Inanna, an Osiris or a Christ, who possesses the deep knowing of death and rebirth.

All our experiences on the road of our journey have prepared us to connect with that inner force, increasing not only our strength and knowledge, but also our self-respect. Once we have achieved this, we are able to feel a strong sense of the power of love that plays an important part. This is love in its widest sense, when uninhibited by fear and self-doubt. Pinocchio loves his father enough to risk his own life for him. Inanna is in love with the force of Life, and is prepared to put her own life on the line to see it return and blossom. The love Beauty eventually forms for the Beast in the fairytale *Beauty and the Beast* turns him back into the prince he had once been. Sacrifice is also very much part of this story, for Beauty has to lose her attachment to her father as a natural part of growing up, and the Beast dies before being reborn as the transformed prince. In one story of the search for the Holy Grail, it is Perceval's love for his king and willingness to sacrifice his own ego in service of that love, which enables the Grail to perform its magic powers of transformation. Life and vitality are restored to both the king and the land itself. A love of life induces us to make a great change that enables us to connect fully with ourselves and with those who care for us.

The transformative process can be a natural part of our development. A young girl once had a dream that involved frogs, symbols of transformation because of their tadpole origins and therefore also symbolic of the change that takes place when we grow from one stage of life to another. In the dream a group of teenagers threw a large number of frogs from a high balcony. As the frogs hit the ground, many of them died. However, the ones that survived mutated into larger frogs, illuminated by coloured lights, and in that moment they acquired the power of speech. The sacrificed frogs were probably all the aspects of childhood that had to be left behind. Even though childhood is a good thing, it naturally has to give way to adulthood. However, the metamorphosis of the frogs that survived not only depicts this transition, but also the magic brought forward from childhood, which deepens with our developing spiritual understanding of the life force.

The theme of sacrifice, death, rebirth and illumination is always central to the transformative pattern. I observed the process of this in a strangely theatrical way in one of my dreams, where an unusual transfiguration took place. A man was dying. His body was grotesquely disfigured and bloated. An invisible force lifted him up into the air. It drew him into the centre of the room, and then absorbed him into the ceiling, which was composed of a soft red fabric. The fabric was then sucked upwards in the centre, like the way sand falls into an hour glass. It opened out into a square shape. This process happened again. The shape of the inside of a small pyramid was being formed in the centre of the ceiling. The third time the material was drawn upwards, I was afraid it would open out to reveal the festering body. However, as the smallest central square opened up, instead of the body, a bright ray of sunshine burst in through the hole and illuminated the entire room with a brilliant white light.

The number three and the transforming Light are seen to be linked as one of the universe's central clues in many mystical traditions. For the Hindus, this is a triad of being, consciousness and divine bliss. For the Taoists it is the "resolving third". It is the resolution of opposites and return to the One. It is the point where male unifies with female to become the Androgen. In the Bible, Light appears on the third day. There are three stages of transformation in alchemy. The first is black, the darkness, the second red, the sacrifice, and the third white, the shining light.

The three stages of transformation express the archetypal experience clearly, from the dark confusion of the labyrinth, through the sacrifice of the monster or the Self, to the final ecstacy of rebirth and release. The rituals of pagan mysteries, such as the Ancient Greek Eleusinian Mysteries that followed the descent and return of the goddess Persephone all went through this process. Plutarch wrote "To die is to be initiated". Initiates went through the experience of dark confusion, followed by a striking moment of terror, before the joyous revelation of a brilliant light.

Shamans of primitive societies, who had gone through extreme pain, were reborn into a world of light and insight, which they could impart to their tribe. They are often referred to as "wounded healers". They plummeted into the depths in order to reach the heights. It is the path taken to move forwards. As Joseph Campbell says in *The Power of Myth*, "One thing that comes out in myths is that at the bottom of the abyss comes the voice of salvation. The black moment is the moment when the real message of transformation is going to come. At the darkest moment comes the light." He also writes in *The Hero with a Thousand Faces*, "every one of us shares the supreme ordeal – carries the cross of the redeemer – not in the bright moments of his tribe's great victories, but in the silences of his personal despair".

In Dave Pelzer's autobiography *The Lost Boy* he describes how in a courtroom he felt the terror of having to face his inner saboteur in front of the mother who had severely abused him. Only he could free himself from her clutches with a few words, but for him these words were deeply painful, because they had to break through the chains of her psychological stranglehold on him. As a child, the psychoanalyst M. Scott Peck also had to confront his inner monster of fear and self-destruction. He came to the realisation that an exclusive educational establishment he was in was crippling him. He then understood that he had to take a huge step into the unknown, away from safety and in the face of serious disapproval. He found that the moment of his greatest despair came just before his revelation, which enabled him to leave.

Our greatest insights often come out of our most desperate moments. We need to search through the dark labyrinths of our complex minds. Then if we can face the pain of letting go of the old outworn or harmful situations and overcome our deepest fear or our most harmful invalidator, we can embrace the unknown and experience the euphoria of a new dawn. Here the Dark Twin presents us with both the terror and the key. As Sharon Heath wrote in the Jungian book *Psychological Perspectives... The Child Within/The Child Without*, "Personal pain and suffering are the midwives to the experience... But look at the child – our lifeblood, our future, our breathtaking beauty. Isn't it worth it? And oh, what joy!"

# The Return

# THE RETURN

"My lord Odysseus," began Teiresias, "you are in search of some easy way to reach your home. But the powers are going to make your journey hard."

Homer – *The Odyssey*

The transformative light of revelation we experience in the heart of the inner realm of our soul journey is the turning point, but we still have to bring this gift of illumination back to the world of consciousness. We need to ensure that we protect the flame, so that nothing can extinguish it, and it can then grow in strength and brightness as we integrate it into our lives.

There are times when the parallel universes are so closely synchronised that the point of inner and outer transformation occurs almost simultaneously. A little girl, who was very unhappy at her school, suffered the situation for a time. However, there came a moment when she suddenly decided that she was not going to put up with it any longer. She made an excuse to go to the cloakroom and then she ran out of the school gates, knowing that she would never return! The outer action occurred so swiftly after the inner transformative decision that apart from the fear of being followed and caught, there was complete clarity in both thought and deed. Luckily, her parents were sympathetic and they found another school for her.

There are legends and myths where the inner and outer transformations happen simultaneously, with all falling into place from that moment onwards. When Persephone is reunited with her mother Demeter, her own personal metamorphosis occurs and the situation is resolved. When a prince kisses the Sleeping Beauty, a joyous celebration and a happy ending follow her awakening. The same thing happens at the end of the fairytale *Snow White*.

However, the point of revelation does not always produce a swift and easy conclusion. More often it is the case that the adventure is not yet over once the inner metamorphosis has occurred. Invariably, there is still the threat of danger or a reversal of the transformative process. Once the inner miracle has taken place, there is still the journey of the return to the conscious realm, so that this process can be outwardly realised. When everything happens in swift succession, it often involves supportive friends, family, partner or spirits, or alternatively it means that the individual has gone through such a deep metamorphosis that the balance and strength built up act as a protection against any further obstructions or threats. But in many instances and stories, the ascent is both dangerous and challenging.

Pinocchio changes inwardly while inside the belly of the whale, the place of death and rebirth, but then he and his father have the hazardous task of finding a way to escape through the whale's jaws. It is only once Pinocchio has saved his father's life at the expense of his own that his outer transformation takes place. Until this point he has continued to have the ass's ears and tale as trademarks of his mistakes, even though he has been displaying courage and a sense of responsibility. Now the good fairy not only revives him and removes the ass's ears and tale, but she also turns him into a real boy.

The myth of Odysseus is another example of a gradual metamorphosis. Odysseus goes through many tests and trials, culminating with his descent into the depths of the Underworld, where he hears the wisdom of the blind seer Teiresias that reveals disturbing truths. Then spirits threaten to pull him down into their domain for good. His survival of this ordeal makes it a transformative experience, but after that he still has to cope with additional obstacles before he can achieve his goal.

As Pinocchio is nearly taken by the whale, Odysseus is almost pulled under by the ravenous whirlpool Charybdis. In both cases, the combination of monstrous forces with the angry waves of the sea give a sense of the potentially overwhelming impact of the disturbed unconscious, before the dry land of conscious rationality is reached. Pinocchio and Odysseus have both gone through a test of faith, ingenuity and wisdom. They have both been tempted off the path of their goal, where their companions were turned into mindless beasts, in Pinocchio's case by Pleasure Island and in Odysseus's by the witch Circe. However, because they have pulled away from these mistakes, they have learned from them as much as from their achievements. In the end, they find the strength to return home without the dependency on their protective forces. Odysseus loses his ship and crew and Pinocchio takes on the parental role as he rescues his father. Our transformation both at the deepest point and on the return needs to be achieved on our own merit, whether we receive assistance or not on the way.

Although at the darkest point we often "see the light", it invariably takes a big effort to build up strength and a sense of self-worth to complete the journey and reach the threshold of our destination at the top of our ascent. In Alcoholics Anonymous, those following the "Twelve Steps" refer to themselves as "recovering alcoholics", rather than "recovered alcoholics". They are aware that their inner demons of fear, laziness, need and depression could take hold at any moment, and they could easily lose their sense of direction, their strength, or the focus of their intuition. In *The Road Less Travelled* M. Scott Peck talks of people who experience an internal revelation and realise that they need to break out of a bad situation. They start therapy, only to curtail it after a short period of time because they cannot bring themselves to see the painful transformative process through.

There was one young man who left the underworld of crime to start afresh, and he began to put his energy into creative pursuits. However, he suddenly disappeared back into that dark hole, because he could not cope with the on-going responsibility of building himself a new life. To go forwards was initially the hard way because he had to work towards carving out a new path, and to rely on his faith that he would succeed in achieving his goal. His old life made him feel important because he had a sense of personal identity with the role he played in his street gang, and because of the instant gratification he received. The excitement of crime made him feel empowered. It was a "quick fix", the easy way.

There are numerous stories of battered wives who come to a realisation of their predicament. However, although they run away from their bullying husbands, and they often seek the help of a refuge, they invariably disappear to return to their bad situation. Logically this makes no sense. They "see the light", leave their "old life", and the warmth of kind and encouraging people surrounds them. However, as if pulled backwards by some invisible magnet, they voluntarily choose to return to a personal hell. This happens because their self-confidence has been undermined, they doubt themselves and they feel unworthy of real love. They invariably mistake the bullying for love, because the abusive partner finds it easy to make them feel guilt, and often employs emotional blackmail. The battered partner can feel indebted. Low self-esteem can also lead one to only feel a sense of personal identity when attached to an apparently powerful figure. The abused have not developed enough confidence to believe that they have the ability to carve out a life of their own, even if at one point they did see the way forward, when they faced the demon of their internal persecutor and tried to make the break.

The ascent towards the outer threshold is literally uphill all the way, so our strength is being severely tested. All our fears from the depths pursue us right up to the entrance. The negative aspect of the Dark Twin is closing in. We are psychologically being worn down. The closer we get to the top, the more susceptible we become to the pressure of our doubts and fears. This is when we are also most vulnerable to outside influences that want to pull us back down. If we are not careful, we can allow ourselves to become their victims.

A tragic situation occurred with the predicament of a young man who had been brought up by a family that constantly wanted to control him and his life. Finally, he made the break by moving away to another country. Here his life began to flower, and for the first time he felt himself to be his own person. However, on visiting his family, he came under their influence again, and he did not return abroad. Eventually, he could not see a way out; he could not bear to tow the family line any longer, but his strength had been sapped away, and he was not able to make the break again. Because of his crippling dilemma, he took his own life. If he had found a way to develop a little more faith in himself, his life could have taken a positive turn.

Suicide curtails further growth in life, but in other cases where there is a failure to find a way, there is still the possibility of another chance. "If only" is a phrase that can lead to a kind of madness with the deep sense of frustration it engenders. However, if that phrase is applied to learning from a mistake so that a similar situation can be changed for the better when it arises, it then becomes a positive guide. It helps to focus the mind on positive solutions, and to give one the strength to complete the important transformations of life.

The qualities of strength, faith and a focus on the vision are all needed for one to hold on to one's sanity when ascending the dangerous path. The deep fears pull from behind like a magnet. The dog and wolf baying in the Moon card of the Tarot pack express the dark shadows of terror that can drag a person into the pit, where the crayfish, symbol of the most primitive demons of the mind, lies in wait. The Moon card also shows how if the monster of terror is survived, the two towers of the threshold are reached. The conscious realm lies beyond. It is at the point of passing between the towers that the next difficult test takes place.

In the story of Orpheus and his wife Eurydice, Hades tells Orpheus that he can lead Eurydice back to the land of the living on the condition that she walks behind him and he does not look back at her at all until they are both out of the Underworld. Orpheus sticks to the bargain as far as the entrance, but as he passes through the portal and the first ray of sunlight falls upon his face, he is suddenly filled with doubt and feels compelled to turn around to check that she is still behind him. But she has not yet left the shadows, so as he looks back, she disappears back into the land of the dead.

Having overcome the terrors of the dark and having achieved his goal with his gift of music and the power of his love, Orpheus loses faith at the last minute. It is the problem of the return threshold. While in the subterranean realm, we may be plagued by terrors, but we are also closely connected to our intuition. For instance, in our dreams we experience fear, but we are also taken along the avenues of vivid symbolism, an eternal flow and expression of the inner knowledge that we all share. The dreamer accepts this without question. One moment he or she is driving a car, and the next is running along the road. The dreamer does not question how the car vanished or where it went, but intuitively knows that it disappeared because he or she is either losing or no longer needing some form of support. When we wake, our rational minds find it strange that we blindly accept apparently irrational situations in dreams. As soon as the light of consciousness hits us, we lose our trust and we question our intuition. We easily let our doubts and anxieties take over. Consciousness alienates us from the pool of essential knowledge we hold within. The illumination we bring up from our inspiration in the depths glows pale in the glaring light of the sun, and if we lose faith that it is there, it is in danger of expiring.

In the stark neon light of modern society, with its materially focussed expectations, the problem of the rationality of consciousness is particularly strong. Like a powerful god, society sets up shining examples for us to aspire towards in the form of successful people, companies and business ventures. While this is in part necessary to our lives and to progress, there is the danger that we can lose respect for our inner knowledge and values. We are under so much pressure to succeed in society's eyes, and we can become so heavily influenced by the greedy ethics of corporations or the subliminal pressures of advertising, that we can become disconnected from our hearts. If this happens, it is as if we have sold our souls. Joseph Campbell sites the evil character of Darth Vader in *Star Wars* as a mythological symbol of this problem, because he is "living not in terms of himself but in terms of an imposed system", an "intentional power". When interviewing Campbell, Bill Moyers realised that this occurs when there is a complete disconnection from the unconscious. He remembered the part in the film when Obi-Wan Kenobi tells Luke Skywalker to turn off his machine, do it himself, and trust his feelings.

Our inner world, which expresses itself through our intuition and our heartfelt feelings, is the real guide that we should follow. If we have enough respect for that and enough faith, balance and focus, we do not stumble with mistrust and we are not blinded to our inner knowledge when the light of consciousness strikes us.

> As dreams that were momentous by night may seem simply silly in the light of day, so the poet and the prophet can discover themselves playing the idiot before a jury of sober eyes.
> Joseph Campbell, *The Hero with a Thousand Faces*

The experience of realising inner truth is always diminished in the world of conscious reality. It is hard enough for one to hold on to ones own revelation, and it is often even harder to transmit that knowledge to the outside world. Sometimes, the frustration can become too intense. Van Gogh committed suicide, partly due to his unstable state of mind, but also because it was so hard for him to find support, understanding and appreciation of his work. He could not find public appreciation of his creative expression in his lifetime. The outside world can be an extremely harsh and ignorant judge.

However, our demons of inner fear and outer mistrust are not the only problem we have to contend with. If we steer too close to the dry land, we are under threat from Scylla, the monster of rationality that threatens to devour our soul-life, but if we are too far into the water, then the monster whirlpool of the unconscious Charybdis threatens to suck us under. In some cases, there is a reluctance to leave the realm of spiritual magic. This can be just as dangerous as the denial of it. There are stories that express this phenomenon, such as *Picnic at Hanging Rock*, in which girls in a state of spiritual ecstasy choose not to return to the world of the living. When Brian Keenan says in *An Evil Cradling*, "to see what was previously invisible is powerfully captivating", he is aware that if he loses his link with reality, then the unconscious could tempt him into a state of insanity.

We are concerned not to lose the connection we have made with the gift of the subterranean realm, particularly if we have discovered the light of insight in the darkest recess, and at the deepest point we have experienced the epiphany of the highest experience. The sense of having connected with the essence of the life force can be intoxicating. As we struggle to regain our personal identity in a new way, we can find ourselves at war within, because we are fighting to hold on to as much as possible of that magical, wider sense of awareness we have just gained. As it cannot all be contained within the constraints of our worldly ego, our very desire to hold on to all the treasures of the deep can threaten to engulf us, thus stopping us from completing the journey.

Those who have been through the near death experience have often spoken of not wanting to return when they were in a clinical state of death. Once they have travelled through a tunnel, or a corresponding image representing a way between two places such as a bridge, and once they have also experienced the Light beyond as the source of knowledge with its all-embracing Love, they resist the subsequent magnetic pull to return to their lives. The experience of the return to the ordinariness and harshness of reality is invariably sharp and emotionally painful. However, although they remain aware of the terrible wrenching moment of loss, they usually speak of a renewed appreciation of life. Having touched on the deeply mystical essence, life's spiritual blood, they realise the value of the gift of life and the need to live life to the full. The power of this mystical experience often gives people a particular special gift that they did not possess before, such as the gift of healing. A taxi driver, who had received the gift of prophecy through a near death experience, astounded people with his accuracy. An invaluable boon is often the recognition of the power of real love for others, for all life, and for oneself as an active part of it. In her book *The Wheel of Life*, Elizabeth Kübler-Ross writes of those who realised through seeing the light that the explanation for the meaning of life is love.

Whether our time in the magical depths is traumatic or ecstatic, we still experience a moment of enlightenment and love at the turning point, which continues to burn in our hearts. It is the light that we should be able to hold on to on our return, for it enables us to see our path, and so to cope with the elements that try to pull us down as we make our difficult ascent. We also need to realise that it is important to see that love is an undercurrent in the conscious world.

Having braved the descent, the terror, the epiphany and the ascent, and having allowed our faith to stand strong at the threshold, we should then be able to apply our gift to our outer lives. However, even that is not easy.

Beyond the Frontiers

# BEYOND THE FRONTIERS

> The more the critical reason dominates, the more impoverished life becomes; but the more of the unconscious, and the more of the myth we are capable of making conscious, the more of life we integrate.
>
> C.G. Jung

Building on our gift of revelation in the conscious world is a difficult task. Having gone through the transformative process, it is not possible to turn the clocks back and live as before, if it is to flourish. Life needs to be handled in a different way to follow the new path with increasing confidence and joy. If we can convince others of our vision, then they share in the benefit of the transformative gift. In fact, it can only work and is only worth while if it is shared, for we are all connected.

However, even if we stand strong when left to our own devices, there are situations where others do not understand. They can be unhelpful and undermining, particularly if they feel threatened by any changes in patterns. For instance, an alcoholic might feel resentful because his friend no longer shares the addiction and is therefore not on the same wavelength as him anymore when they meet in the pub, and consequently they are not meeting there as often as they used to. People can attempt to enforce their will when they are losing control. In the film *Fried Green Tomatoes* a middle aged woman, who has been dominated and abused by her husband for years, is helped by an old lady to gain the strength to become her own person. Initially, the husband is appalled by this transformation and expresses his rage, but because the wife holds firm, he eventually gives in. He then also goes through a transformation and becomes a much more positive person. Another character in the film finds that she has to leave her husband because he remains unable to accept her wish to change so that she can flower to her potential.

As the Black Sheep chapter explores, people can feel threatened by anyone they do not understand, which includes those who appear to be different because of their transformation. Suspicion and jealousy can be evoked.

Helen Keller is an example of someone who had to brave the storms of resentment and misunderstanding. She went through a remarkable transformation from a painful, icy cold world of total darkness, without being able to either see or hear, to an illuminated world where she could speak, communicate with others and understand the most complex of concepts. She was even able to know what colour a thing was by feeling vibrations that would be imperceptible to most people. She had a strong empathy with the sufferings of others and a deep sense of the joy of life. She felt compelled to share her feelings and her transformative experience with the outer world. In *A Mythic Life* Jean Houston describes how Helen and her teacher Annie were met with opposition and suffered from a number of accusations, ranging from faking her experiences to the intervention of bad spirits. However, despite all the problems she was up against, Helen rose above the antagonism. With the light of the transfiguration she had experienced, she was able to become a beacon of light in her support for the handicapped and in the message of compassion and positive hope she gave to the world. She recognised the force of love as the essence of Life, and that when this force runs freely through our hearts, we feel joy and a sense of oneness with others. We are then much more able to overcome both outer and inner blocks and difficulties, and it is more possible for us to reach out to help those in need around us. Helen Keller opened up her doors of perception as the light of love and positivity flooded into her dark world, igniting the brightness of her inner eyes.

As "The Inspiration of Childhood" chapter explores, small children see things with new eyes, which enables them to feel the magical essence of life. If adults can do this through the wonder of transformation, then their insights are deeply rewarding for both themselves and for those they communicate with. It can also be an encouragement for others to find the magic inside themselves. Otherwise, there is a danger that the most enlightened of messages can go stale as time passes by, particularly if tampered with by people with personal ambition, fear or prejudice. Religion often suffers from this kind of contamination. Spirituality needs to constantly replenish itself and grow with an ever-deeper understanding. Each generation and as many individuals as possible need to have a direct experience of the life blood of the spirit, so that in whatever form we choose to interpret it, its essence is kept alive.

The jewels of inspiration discovered in the past are the eternal gifts of our development, but dust gathers with the passing of time if we just look upon these without going back to the source ourselves. If a pond becomes stagnant, it grows thick with algae, and eventually it is no longer able to sustain the myriad of life forms it once did.

We see the need for constant renewal in every aspect of Nature. In the depths of the Earth, it is still an active living force, where molten rock moves and pushes its way towards the surface. Volcanic eruptions can be catastrophic, but they renew the face of the Earth with life-blood from below. Although the lava solidifies, it produces a particularly fertile soil. It has recently been discovered that the Earth once suffered an ice age, which was so severe that ice eventually covered the whole planet. It was the heat and gasses from volcanoes that eventually melted the ice. Planets that no longer "bleed" are sometimes referred to as "dead planets". Current information suggests that Mars, which scientists believe once sustained life, is one of these planets. Nature, and indeed the whole universe, is in constant need of movement and renewal for life to be sustained and developed. As part of the life process, our development follows the same pattern. As Fritjof Capra noted in his book *The Tao of Physics,* all matter is part of a continuous cosmic dance.

The truth of mystical experience is reflected in the universe. There is no separation between the spiritual and material universes in the fundamental patterns of life. It is the ecstatic dance of being. The psychologist Carl Rogers once likened the peak of scientific knowledge to a mystical peak experience. Mother Nature provides more than just an analogy for any essential spiritual truth. Likewise, the macrocosm of the wider cosmos is reflected in the microcosm of our inner worlds. We see cosmic patterns that reveal how the need for death, rebirth and periodical change and renewal goes hand in hand with the wonder of creativity and evolving new forms of life.

In *What is the Universe In?* Anthony Grey states, "All life must be relative". The science writer John Gribbin has put forward a theory of evolution of universes that is based on the clues of the universe. He believes that the universe is alive and that it could be a development from a previous one, as a baby is a mutated form of its parent. The idea is that whatever the scale, the same pattern is followed, from the widest picture imaginable to the microscopic universe within ourselves.

If we are in tune with the cosmos, both psychologically and spiritually, we go through a continuous process of evolution. We journey into the labyrinth many times, each visit being a part of one long voyage of growth and discovery. We learn and grow through our mistakes as well as our successes, and we constantly return to the point of transformation, but each time at a higher level. When life's experience is in flow, it develops like a rising spiral. At each point of death and rebirth, we once again pass through the Dark Twin's gate of transformative experience and back into the Light. If we are not willing to go through this dark portal at any given stage, then we are stuck in a groove and we are not able to continue our journey until we find a way through. Fighting any feelings of fear, hopelessness, rigid pride or hatred, we combat the threat of stagnancy.

The creative journey, in which we become the heroes or heroines of our dreams, is our destiny in the deepest sense of the word. It is not fixed, as we come across many crossroads, many choices, and many different ways in which to walk each path we choose. But if we are to follow our respective destinies, we need strength and faith, the guidance of our intuition and an open and loving heart. Our journey has no end. It is an adventure that is constantly unfolding, with each layer being more vibrant, creative and alive than the one before. Our path is to keep moving through the spiral labyrinth, inward to enable our hearts to reach out to others, forwards to the place we originally came from, and downwards to reach the higher levels of spirit.

Our destiny lies within the realm of the Dark Twin, as it is a paradox. It is the gift the Dark Twin presents us as the dark aspect of the universal life force, which lies within all of us. Our role is important because as we face pain and express our love and as we push through boundaries and grow, we enrich the universal spirit. In our role as co-creators we enable it to flower and to manifest itself through the myriad of forms. Through the power of its inspiration, it encourages us to bring into focus a sense of the wonder of our potential. We are all capable of both tapping into and adding to the infinite source of knowledge. Both physically and spiritually, we are stardust. We are individually unique, which is how each of us is like a deity with his or her own special role, yet along with everything that lives, we are all connected as part of one spirit. We are all involved with the creative process of the life force, and the Dark Twin holds the key to that great mystery.

# THE END

# Acknowledgements

I would like to thank Tony Grey for his inspired ideas and for enabling this book to come to fruition, Jenny Smith for her useful suggestions, and Harry Pearce for his invaluable help and original cover design. I am also particularly grateful to Amanda Lehmann for her patience and hard work, Ann Goodwin for her time, love and encouragement; John Goodwin and Steve Hackett for all their support.

## Permissions Acknowledgements

Grateful acknowledgement is made to the following for permission to reprint previously published material:

HarperCollins Publishers, Inc.: Extract from A MYTHIC LIFE by Jean Houston published by HarperCollins Inc. 1995. Used by permission of HarperCollins Publishers, Inc.

HarperCollins Publishers Ltd.: Extract from DICTIONARY OF SYMBOLS by Tom Chetwynd, Copyright © 1982 Tom Chetwynd. Published by Paladin Books in 1982 and by Aquarian Press in 1993. Used by permission of HarperCollins Publishers Ltd.

Extract from MEMORIES, DREAMS, REFLECTIONS by C. G. Jung. Copyright © Random House Inc. 1961. Published by Fontana Press 1995. Used by permission of HarperCollins Publishers Ltd.

Extract from ENTERING THE CIRCLE by Olga Kharitidi, Copyright © 1996 Olga Kharitidi. Published by HarperSanFrancisco in 1996 and by Thorsons in 1997. Used by permission of HarperCollins Publishers Ltd.

Extract from SEVENTY-EIGHT DEGREES OF WISDOM; A BOOK OF TAROT by Rachel Pollack, Copyright © 1983 Rachel Pollack. Published by Aquarian Press in 1983. Used by permission of HarperCollins Publishers Ltd.

Hodder and Stoughton: Extract from R. D. LAING: A DIVIDED SELF by John Clay. Published by Hodder and Stoughton in 1996. Reproduced by permission of Hodder and Stoughton Limited.

Extract from DARK NATURE by Lyall Watson. Published in 1995 by Hodder and Stoughton. Reproduced by permission of Hodder and Stoughton Limited.

C.S. Lewis Company: THE LAST BATTLE by C. S. Lewis copyright © C. S. Lewis Pte. Ltd. 1956; THE LION, THE WITCH AND THE WARDROBE by C. S. Lewis copyright © C. S. Lewis Pte. Ltd. 1950; THE MAGICIAN'S NEPHEW by C. S. Lewis copyright © C. S. Lewis Pte. Ltd. 1955; SURPRISED BY JOY BY C. S. Lewis copyright © C. S. Lewis Pte. Ltd. 1955. Extracts reprinted by permission of the C. S. Lewis Company.

Penguin Books Ltd.: Extract from THE MYTH OF THE GODDESS by Anne Baring and Jules Cashford, Copyright © Anne Baring and Jules Cashford 1991. Published by Viking in 1991. Quotations: p. 163 and p. 674 of Penguin Books London edition, 1993. Reproduced by permission of Penguin Books Ltd.

Princeton University Press: Extract from THE HERO WITH A THOUSAND FACES by Joseph Campbell. Copyright © 1949 by Bollingen Foundation Inc., New York. First Princeton/Bollingen paperback printing, 1972. Used by permission of Princeton University Press.

Extract from THE SYMBOLIC QUEST by Edward C. Whitmont. Copyright © 1969 by the C. G. Jung Foundation for Analytical Psychology. New material copyright © 1991 by Edward C. Whitmont. First hardcover edition by G. P. Putnam's Sons for the C. G. Jung Foundation for Analytical Psychology. First Princeton Paperback printing, 1972. Used by permission of Princeton University Press.

The Random House Group: Extract from ILLUSIONS by Richard Bach published by Rider. Used by permission of The Random

# Works cited

**[ ] = original publication date**

**Part One: The Essential Nature of the Dark Twin**

### Chapter One: The Dark Twin's Power
Campbell, Joseph with Bill Moyers: *The Power of Myth.* New York: Doubleday Publishing, 1988, p. 161.
Pollack, Rachel: *Seventy-Eight Degrees of Wisdom.* Wellingborough, UK: The Aquarian Press Limited, 1984, p. 70.

### Chapter Two: Twins of Darkness and Light
Baring, Anne and Jules Cashford: *The Myth of the Goddess.* London: Arkana-Penguin Books, 1993, p. 674.
Blake, William: *The Marriage of Heaven and Hell.* 1790.
Campbell, Joseph: *The Hero with a Thousand Faces.* New Jersey: Bollingen Series/Princeton, 1973 [1949].
Daniel, Samuel: *Delia,* sonnet 54, 1592.
Euripides: *The Bacchae.* c. 406 BC.
Gibran, Kahlil: *The Prophet.* Hertfordshire: Wordsworth Editions Limited, 1996 [1923], p. 30.
Houston, Jean: *A Mythic Life.* New York: Harper Collins, 1996, p. 322.
Rilke, Rainer Maria: Letter to a Polish translator.
Woolger, Jennifer Barker and Roger J. Woolger: *The Goddess Within.* London: Rider, 1993, p. 242.

### Chapter Three: The Black Sheep
Anderson, Hans Christian: *The Ugly Duckling.* 1844.
Brontë, Emily: *Wuthering Heights.* 1847.
Campbell, Joseph with Bill Moyers: *The Power of Myth.* New York: Doubleday Publishing, 1988, p. 142.
Keenan, Brian: *An Evil Cradling.* London: Vintage, Arrow, 1993, p. 95.
Laing, R. D.: *Wisdom, Madness and Folly.* Macmillan, 1985.
Shelley, Mary: *Frankenstein.* 1818.
Straparola, Gianfrancesco: *Beauty and the Beast.* First Collected in *The Nights of Straparola,* 1550-53. Other early versions: Madam de Villeneuve, Perrault.
Swift, Jonathan, 1739.
Whitmont, Edward C.: *The Symbolic Quest.* New Jersey, USA/ Chichester, UK: Princeton University Press, 1991, p. 264.

**Chapter Four: The Trickster**
Chetwynd, Tom: *Dictionary of Symbols*. London: Aquarian Press, 1993, p. 407.
Grimm, Jacob and Wilhelm: *Hansel and Gretel*. Nineteenth century.
Keenan, Brian: *An Evil Cradling*. London: Vintage, Arrow, 1993, p. 81.
Jung, C. G.: *Four Archetypes*. London: Ark Paperbacks, 1992 [1959], p. 143.
Plato (429-347 BC).
Shakespeare, William: *A Midsummer Night's Dream*.
Shakespeare, William: *King Lear*.
Shakespeare, William: *Macbeth*.
Wood, Michael: *In Search of the Trojan War*. London: BBC, 1985.

**Chapter Five: The Dark Force in Nature**
Carlyle, Thomas: *Past and Present*. 1843.
Conrad, Joseph: *Heart of Darkness*. UK: Penguin Books, 1985 [1902], pp. 69, 111.
Golding, William: *Lord of the Flies*. London: Faber and Faber Limited, 1954.
Gribbin, John: *Space*. London: BBC, 2001.
Mowat, Farley: *Never Cry Wolf*. Ontario, Canada: McClelland and Stewart Limited, 1963.
Shakespeare, William: *King Lear*.
Watson, Lyall: *Dark Nature*. London: Hodder and Stoughton, 1995.

**Chapter Six: The Dark Force in its Constructive Role**
Gibran, Kahlil: *The Prophet*. Hertfordshire: Wordsworth Editions Limited, 1996 [1923], p. 32.
Shakespeare, William: *Hamlet*.

**Chapter Seven: The Dark Force as Pure Destruction**
Ende, Michael: *The Never Ending Story*. UK: Allen Lane, 1983 [1979].
Shakespeare, William: *Macbeth*.
Watson, Lyall: *Dark Nature*. London: Hodder and Stoughton, 1995, p. 202.

**Chapter Eight: How Evil is Born**
Attenborough, David, directed film: *Cry Freedom*. 1987.
Cooper, J. C.: *Yin and Yang*. Northamptonshire, UK: The Aquarian Press, 1981, p. 61.
Forster, E. M.: *Howards End*. Edward Arnold, 1910.
Milton, John: *Paradise Lost*. 1667.

Peck, M. Scott: *Further along the Road less Travelled.* London: Simon & Schuster Ltd., 1993.

Shakespeare, William: *Sonnet 94.*

Stevenson, Robert Louis: *Dr. Jekyll and Mr. Hyde.* 1886.

**Chapter Nine: Compassion**

Gibran, Kahlil: *The Prophet.* Hertfordshire, UK: Wordsworth Editions Limited, 1996 [1923], p. 9.

Leakey, Richard: *The Making of Mankind.* London: Michael Joseph Limited, 1981, pp. 245-246.

Seattle, Chief: An appeal to the Washington government, 1854.

Watson, Lyall: *Dark Nature.* London: Hodder and Stoughton, 1995.

**Chapter Ten: Passion**

Brontë, Emily: *Wuthering Heights.* 1847.

Dante: *Divine Comedy.* 1306-1321.

Gibran, Kahlil: *The Prophet.* Hertfordshire, UK: Wordsworth Editions Limited, 1996 [1923], p.6.

Keenan, Brian: *An Evil Cradling.* London: Vintage, Arrow, 1993.

**Chapter Eleven: Creativity**

Blake, William: Letter to Dr. Trusler. 1799.

Blake, William: *The Marriage of Heaven and Hell.* 1790.

Estés, Clarissa Pinkola: *Women who run with the Wolves.* London: Rider, 1995, p. 317.

Grey, Anthony: *What is the Universe In?* Norwich, UK: Tagman Worldwide Ltd., 2003, p. 123. Originally: *A Man Alone.* London: Michael Joseph Ltd., 1971.

Lewis, Clive Staples: *Surprised by Joy.* UK: Fount Paperbacks, 1984 [1955], p. 93.

Lewis, Clive Staples: *The Last Battle.* UK: The Bodley Head, 1956.

Paracelsus (doctor interested in alchemy and the way of nature, sixteenth century).

Taplin, Oliver: *Greek Fire.* London: Jonathan Cape Ltd., 1989, p. 97.

Wells, Orson, directed film: *Citizen Caine.* 1941.

Wordsworth, William: *Preface to Lyrical Ballads.* 1807.

**Chapter Twelve: The Inspiration of Childhood**

Baudelaire, Charles: *The Painter of Modern Life and other Essays,* trans. and ed. Jonathan Mayne. London: Phaidon Press, 1964 [1863], p.8.

Clay, John: *R. D. Laing.* London: Hodder and Stoughton, 1996, p. 216.

Defoe, Daniel: *Robinson Crusoe.* 1719.

Lewis, Clive Staples: *The Lion, the Witch and the Wardrobe*. UK: Penguin books, 1973 [1950], reference to story and message to Lucy Barfield.


## Part Two: Venturing into the Dark Twin's Realm

### Chapter One: Preparing for the journey
Adams, Henry Brooks: *The Education of Henry Adams*. 1907.
Eliot, Thomas Stearns: *Little Gidding*, Section Five, last of his Four Quartets. London: Faber and Faber Ltd., 2001 [1943].

### Chapter Two: The Parallel Universe
Baum, L. Frank: *The Wizard of Oz*. 1900.
Chetwynd, Tom: *Dictionary of Symbols*. London: Aquarian Press, 1993 [1982], p. 411.
Jung, C. G.: *Memories, Dreams, Reflections*. London: Fontana Press/Harper Collins Publishers, 1995 [1961].
Lewis, Clive Staples: *The Magician's Nephew*. Harmondsworth, UK: Penguin Books Ltd./Puffin Books, 1973 [1955], p. 50.
Origen [Third century AD].
Peck, M. Scott: *Further along the Road less Travelled*. London: Simon & Schuster Ltd., 1993.
Shakespeare, William: *Julius Caesar*.

### Chapter Three: The Threshold
Baring, Anne and Jules Cashford: *The Myth of the Goddess*. London: Arkana-Penguin Books, 1993, p. 163.

### Chapter Four: Helpful Spirits
Houston, Jean: *A Mythic Life*. New York: Harper Collins, 1996, p. 135.

### Chapter Five: The Inner Spirit
Kharitidi, Olga: *Entering the Circle*. London: Harper Collins, 1997, pp. 71, 72, 138.
Lewis, Clive Staples: *The Great Divorce*. UK: Fontana, 1977 [1946].

### Chapter Six: Ride the Wild Tiger
Keenan, Brian: *An Evil Cradling*. London: Vintage, Arrow, 1993, p. 79.
*Ride the Wild Tiger*: Unknown.

**Chapter Seven: Letting Go**
Estés, Clarissa Pinkola: *Women who run with the Wolves.* London: Rider, 1995, p. 252.
Gibran, Kahlil: *The Prophet.* Hertfordshire, UK: Wordsworth Editions Limited, 1996 [1923], p. 8.
Grey, Anthony: *Hostage in Peking Plus.* Norwich, UK: Tagman Worldwide Limited, 2003 [1970].
Keenan, Brian: *An Evil Cradling.* London: Vintage, Arrow, 1993.
Peck, M. Scott: *The Road less Travelled.* London: Arrow, 1990, p. 143.

**Chapter Eight: Taking the Plunge**
Brontë, Charlotte: *Jane Eyre.* 1847.
Peck, M. Scott: *The Road less Travelled.* London: Arrow, 1990, p. 149.
Pollack, Sydney, directed film: *Out of Africa.* 1985.

**Chapter Nine: The Way**
Baum, L. Frank: *The Wizard of Oz.* 1900.
Houston, Jean: *A Mythic Life.* New York: Harper Collins, 1996, p. 146.
Jung, C. G. and M. L. von Franz: *Man and his Symbols.* London: Picador, 1978 [1964], p. 235.
Keenan, *Brian: An Evil Cradling.* London: Vintage, Arrow, 1993, p. 81.
Lewis, Clive Staples: *The Last Battle.* UK: Penguin Books, 1967 [1956], p. 163.

**Chapter Ten: Breaking into the Inner Sanctum**
Campbell, Joseph with Bill Moyers: *The Power of Myth.* New York: Doubleday Publishing, 1988, p. 149.
Gibran, Kahlil: *The Prophet.* Hertfordshire, UK: Wordsworth Editions Limited, 1996 [1923], p. 32.
Pollack, Rachel: *Seventy-Eight Degrees of Wisdom.* Wellingborough, UK: The Aquarian press Limited, 1984, p. 105.
Tolkien, J. R. R.: *The Lord of the Rings.* London: George Allen & Unwin Ltd., 1966 [1954, 1955]

**Chapter Eleven: A Message of Transformation**
Bach, Richard: *Illusions.* London: Arrow, 1998, p. 134.
Book of Jonah, Bible: *Jonah and the Whale.* Landoll, 1999.
Campbell, Joseph: *The Hero with a Thousand Faces.* New Jersey, USA: Princeton/Bollingen Printing, 1973 [1949], p. 391.
Campbell, Joseph with Bill Moyers: *The Power of Myth.* New York: Doubleday Publishing, 1988, p. 37.
Collodi, Carlo: *Pinocchio.* 1883.

Heath, Sharon (wrote the first chapter and co-edited with Ernest Lawrence Rossi): *Psychological Perspectives.* Issue 21. The C. G. Jung Institute of Los Angeles, 1989, p.10.

Hesse, Hermann: *Demian.* London: Picador, 1995 [1958], p. 112.

Kharitidi, Olga: *Entering the Circle.* London: Harper Collins, 1997, p. 136.

Pelzer, Dave: *The Lost Boy.* USA: Orion Media, 2000.

Straparola, Gianfrancesco: *Beauty and the Beast.* First collected in *The Nights of Straparola*, 1550-53. Other early versions: madam Villeneuve, Perrault.

Tolkien, J. R. R.: *The Lord of the Rings.* London: George Allen & Unwin Ltd., 1966 [1954,1955].

Whitmont, Edward C.: *The Symbolic Quest.* New Jersey, USA/ Chichester, UK: Princeton University Press, 1991, p. 307.

Wilcox, Fred M. directed film: *Forbidden Planet,* 1956.

**Chapter Twelve: The Return**

Campbell, Joseph: *The Hero with a Thousand Faces.* New Jersey, USA: Princeton/Bollingen Printing, 1973 [1949], p. 218.

Campbell, Joseph with Bill Moyers: *The Power of Myth.* New York: Doubleday Publishing, 1998, p. 114.

Collodi, Carlo: *Pinocchio.* 1883.

Grimm, Jacob and Wilhelm: *Sleeping Beauty.* Nineteenth century.

Grimm, Jacob and Wilhelm: *Snow White.* Nineteenth century.

Homer: *The Odyssey,* c. 700 BC.

Keenan, Brian: *An Evil Cradling.* London: Vintage, Arrow, 1993, p. 81.

Kübler-Ross, Elizabeth: *The Wheel of Life.* UK: Bantam Press, 1997.

Lindsay, Joan: *Picnic at Hanging Rock.* UK: Penguin Books Ltd., 1970 [1967].

Peck, M. Scott: *The Road less Travelled.* London: Arrow, 1990.

**Chapter Thirteen: Beyond the Frontiers**

Arnet, John, directed film: *Fried Green Tomatoes.* 1991.

Capra, Fritjof: *The Tao of Physics.* Flamingo, 1992 [1975].

Grey, Anthony: *What is the Universe In?* Norwich, UK: Tagman Worldwide (Ltd.), 2003, p. 35. Originally: *A Man Alone.* London: Michael Joseph Ltd., 1971.

Gribbin, John: *Space.* London: BBC, 2001.

Houston, Jean: *A Mythic Life.* New York: Harper Collins, 1996, pp. 118-119.

Jung C. G.: *Memories, Dreams, Reflections.* London: Fontana Press, Harper Collins, 1995 [1961], p. 333.

# Selected Bibliography

**| | = original publication date**

Anderson, Hans Christian: *The Complete Hans Christian Anderson.* Editor: Lilly Owens. Gramercy Books, 1993.

Baring, Anne and Jules Cashford: *The Myth of the Goddess.* London: Arkana-Penguin Books, 1993.

Baudelaire, Charles: *The Painter of Modern Life and Other Essays.* Translated and edited by Jonathan Mayne. London: Phaidon Press, 1964 [1863].

Baum, L. Frank: *The Wizard of Oz.* UK: Penguin, 1995 [1900].

Bettelheim, Bruno: *The Uses of Enchantment.* UK: Penguin, 1978 [Thames & Hudson, 1976].

Brontë, Charlotte: *Jane Eyre.* UK: Penguin, 2003 [1847].

Brontë, Emily: *Wuthering Heights.* UK: Penguin, 2004 [1847].

Campbell, Joseph: *The Hero with a Thousand Faces.* New Jersey, USA: Bollingen Series/Princeton, 1973 [1949].

Campbell, Joseph with Bill Moyers: *The Power of Myth.* New York: Doubleday Publishing, 1988.

Capra, Fritjof: *The Tao of Physics.* Flamingo, 1992 [1975].

Carlyle Thomas: *Past and Present.* Ed: Richard D. Altick. New York University Press, 1977 [1843].

Chetwynd, Tom: *Dictionary of Symbols.* London: Aquarian Press, 1993.

Clay, John: *R. D. Laing.* London: Hodder and Stoughton, 1996.

Collodi, Carlo: *Pinocchio.* Walker Books, 2003 [1883].

Conrad, Joseph: *Heart of Darkness.* UK: Penguin Books, 1985 [1902].

Cooper, J. C.: *Yin and Yang.* Northamptonshire, UK: The Aquarian Press, 1981.

Daniel, Samuel: *Delia.* Scholar P, 1969.

Dante, Alighieri, et al.: *Divine Comedy.* Oxford Paperbacks, 1998.

Davis, Michael: *William Blake, A New Kind of Man.* UK: Paul Elek Limited, 1977.

Defoe, Daniel: *Robinson Crusoe.* Oxford Paperbacks, 1998 [1719].

Eliot, T. S.: *Little Gidding,* Section Five, last of his *Four Quartets.* London: Faber and Faber Ltd., 2001 [1943].

Ende, Michael: *The Never Ending Story.* UK: Allen Lane, 1983 [1979].

Estés, Clarissa Pinkola: *Women who run with the Wolves.* London: Rider, 1995.

Euripides: *The Bacchae and Other Plays.* UK: Penguin Books, 1980 [c. 406 BC].

Evans, Cooper (editor): *Beauty and the Beast.* Green Tiger Press, 1989 [In Gianfrancesco Straparola's *Nights of Straparola*, 1550-53. Other versions: Madam de Villeneuve, Perrault].

Forster, E. M.: *Howards End.* UK: Penguin, 1978 [1910].

Garrett, Eileen: *Many Voices: The Autobiography of a Medium.* New York: G. P. Putnam's, 1968.

Gibran, Kahlil: *The Prophet.* Hertfordshire, UK: Wordsworth Editions Limited, 1996 [1923].

Golding, William: *Lord of the Flies.* London: Faber and Faber Limited, 1954.

Grey, Anthony: *Hostage in Peking Plus.* Norwich, UK: Tagman Worldwide Ltd., 2003 [1970].

Grey, Anthony: *What is the Universe In?* Norwich, UK: Tagman Worldwide Ltd., 2003. Originally: *A Man Alone.* London: Michael Joseph Ltd., 1971.

Gribbin, John: *Space.* London: BBC, 2001.

Grimm, Jacob and Wilhelm: *The Complete Brothers Grimm Fairy Tales.* Editor: Lilly Owens. Avenel Books, 1981.

Hall, Manly P.: *Paracelsus: His Mystical and Medical Philosophy.* US: Philosophical Research Society, 1989.

Heath, Sharon (wrote the first chapter and co-edited with Ernest Lawrence Rossi): *Psychological Perspectives*, Issue 21. The C. G. Jung Institute of Los Angeles, 1989.

Hesse, Hermann: *Demian.* London: Picador, 1995 [1958].

Homer: *The Odyssey.* Penguin Classics, 1980.

Houston, Jean: *A Mythic Life.* New York: Harper Collins, 1996.

Jung, C. G.: *Dreams.* London: Ark, 1993 [First published in UK: 1982].

Jung, C. G.: *Four Archetypes.* London: Ark Paperbacks, 1992 [1959].

Jung, C. G.: *Man and his Symbols.* London: Picador, 1978 [1964].

Jung, C. G.: *Memories, Dreams, Reflections.* London: Fontana Press/Harper Collins Publishers, 1995 [1961].

Kalweit, Holger: *Dreamtime and Inner Space.* Boston, US: Shambhala Publications, Inc., 1988.

Keenan, Brian: *An Evil Cradling.* London: Vintage, Arrow, 1993.

Keller, Helen: *The Story of my Life.* Signet Classics, 2002.

Kerényi, C.: *The Gods of the Greeks.* London: Thames and Hudson, 1976 [1951].

Keynes, Geoffrey: *The Complete Writings of William Blake.* London: Oxford Standard Authors Edition, 1969 [1966].

Kharitidi, Olga: *Entering the Circle.* London: Thorsons/Harper Collins, 1997.

Kübler-Ross, Elizabeth: *The Wheel of Life.* UK: Bantam Press, 1997.

Laing, R. D.: *The Politics of Experience and the Bird of Paradise.* Penguin Books, 1990 [1967].

Laing, R. D.: *Wisdom, Madness and Folly.* London: Macmillan, 1985.

Leakey, Richard: *The Making of Mankind.* London: Michael Joseph Limited, 1981.

Lewis, Clive Staples: *Surprised by Joy.* UK: Fount Paperbacks, 1984 [1955].

Lewis, Clive Staples: *The Complete Chronicles of Narnia.* London: Collins, 1998.

Lewis, Clive Staples: *The Great Divorce.* UK: Fontana, 1977 [1946].

Lewis, Clive Staples: *The Last Battle.* Harmondsworth, UK: Penguin, 1967 [1956].

Lewis, Clive Staples: *The Lion, the Witch & the Wardrobe.* Harmondsworth, UK: Penguin, 1973 [1950].

Lewis, Clive Staples: *The Magician's Nephew.* Harmondsworth, UK: Penguin, 1973 [1955].

Lindsay, Joan: *Picnic at hanging Rock.* UK: Penguin Books Ltd., 1970 (1967).

Maybury-Lewis, David: *Millennium: Tribal Wisdom in the Modern World.* US: Viking Penguin, 1992.

Milton, John: *Paradise Lost.* Oxford World's Classics, 2004.

Mowat, Farley: *Never Cry Wolf.* Ontario, Canada: McClelland & Stewart Limited, 1963.

Peat, F. David: *Blackfoot Physics.* London: Fourth Estate, 1996.

Peck, M. Scott: *Further along the Road less Travelled.* London: Simon & Schuster Ltd., 1993.

Peck, M. Scott: *The Road less Travelled.* London: Arrow, 1990.

Pelzer, Dave: *A Child called It.* USA: Orion Media, 2000.

Pelzer, Dave: *The Lost Boy.* USA: Orion Media, 2000.

Pollack, Rachel: *Seventy-Eight Degrees of Wisdom.* Wellingborough, UK: The Aquarian Press Limited, 1984.

Seattle, Chief: *Brother Eagle, Sister Sky: A Message from Chief Seattle.* Illustrated by Susan Jeffers. Puffin Books, 2004 [Appeal to the Washington government, 1854].

Shakespeare, William: *Complete Works of Shakespeare.* Editor: Howard Staunton. Wordsworth Editions Ltd., 1996.

Shelley, Mary: *Frankenstein.* UK: Penguin, 1994 [1818].

Spiri, Johanna: *Heidi.* UK: Penguin, 1956 [1880].

Stevenson, Robert Louis: *Dr. Jekyll and Mr. Hyde.* UK: Penguin, 2004 [1886].

Taplin, Oliver: *Greek Fire.* London: Jonathan Cape Ltd., 1989.

Tolkien, J. R. R.: *The Lord of the Rings.* London: George Allen & Unwin Ltd., 1966 [1954, 1955].

Tucker, Michael: *Dreaming with Open Eyes.* Aquarian/Harper San Francisco, 1992.

Watson, Lyall: *Dark Nature.* London: Hodder and Stoughton, 1995.

Whitmont, Edward C.: *The Symbolic Quest.* New Jersey, US/ Chichester, UK: Princeton University Press, 1991.

Wood, Michael: *In Search of the Trojan War.* London: BBC, 1985.

Woolger, Jennifer Barker and Roger J. Woolger: *The Goddess Within.* London: Rider, 1993.

Wordsworth, William and Samuel Taylor Coleridge: *Lyrical Ballads: With a few other poems.* Penguin books Ltd., 1999 [1807].

Wydenbruck, N.: *Rilke: Man and Poet.* London: John Lehmann, 1949.

**Tagman**

# OTHER BOOKS BY THE TAGMAN PRESS

**Dr Batmanghelidj**
Your Body's Many Cries for Water ISBN 1-903571-49-9
Water & Salt: Your Healers from Within ISBN 1-903571-24-3
Water Cures, Drugs Kill ISBN 1-903571-33-2
Eradicate Asthma Now, with Water! ISBN 1-903571-35-9
How to deal with Back Pain ISBN 1-903571-29-4
Obesity, Cancer & Depression: ISBN 1-903571-54-5
How water can cure these deadly diseases

**Anthony Grey**
Hostage in Peking Plus ISBN 1-903571-11-1
What is the Universe in? ISBN 1-903571-12-X
Saigon Vol 1 ISBN 1-903571-50-2
Saigon Vol 2 ISBN 1-903571-51-0
The Prime Minister was a Spy – 2005 ISBN 1-903571-38-3

**Ray & Gillian Brown with Paul Dickson**
A Mere Grain of Sand ISBN 1-903571-47-2

**Rael**
The Final Message ISBN 0-9530921-1-9
Lets Welcome the Extra-Terrestrials ISBN 1-903571-28-6
Sensual Meditation ISBN 1-903571-07-3
Yes to Human Cloning ISBN 1-903571-05-7

**Vonnie Bloom – Yoga CDs**
Relax for Health ISBN 1-903571-27-8
Stretch for Health ISBN 1-903571-26-X

**To order any of the above please call our
Credit Card Hotline on 0845 644 4186
or visit our website and order online
www.tagman-press.com**

# Biography

Joanna Lehmann received a BA in Drama and Classics at London University, and specialised in both Ancient Greek Religion and in-depth character study. She has acted and directed in theatre and has worked on various film and video projects. These include *Soulscapes,* an allegorical film about personal discovery, and *Change of Heart,* a short film about a young man who finds a positive alternative to crime. She is about to have a book published that studies the nature of rebellion. She writes articles on psychology, spirituality, mythology and the supernatural for various publications and draws these elements together in *Our Dark Twin* as a venture into the realm of mind and soul.

Printed in the United Kingdom
by Lightning Source UK Ltd.
108428UKS00001B/91-207